I0536622

DISCLAIMER

The author and publisher are providing this book and its contents on an "as is" basis and make no representations or warranties of any kind with respect to this book or its contents. The author and publisher disclaim all such representations and warranties, including but not limited to warranties of merchantability. In addition, the author and publisher do not represent or warrant that the information accessible via this book is accurate, complete, or current.

Except as specifically stated in this book, neither the author nor publisher, nor any authors, contributors, or other representatives will be liable for damages arising out of or in connection with the use of this book. This is a comprehensive limitation of liability that applies to all damages of any kind, including (without limitation) compensatory; direct, indirect, or consequential damages; loss of data, income, or profit; loss of or damage to property; and claims of third parties.

This Book Comes With Free Bonus Puzzles

Available Here:

BestActivityBooks.com/WSBONUS20

5 TIPS TO START!

1) HOW TO SOLVE

The Puzzles are in a Classic Format:

- Words are hidden without breaks (no spaces, dashes, ...)
- Orientation: Forward & Backward, Up & Down or in Diagonal (can be in both directions)
- Words can overlap or cross each other

2) ACTIVE LEARNING

To encourage learning actively, a space is provided next to each word to write down the translation. The **DICTIONARY** allows you to verify and expand your knowledge. You can look up and write down each translation, find the words in the Puzzle then add them to your vocabulary!

3) TAG YOUR WORDS

Have you tried using a tag system? For example, you could mark the words which have been difficult to find with a cross, the ones you loved with a star, new words with a triangle, rare words with a diamond and so on...

4) ORGANIZE YOUR LEARNING

We also offer a convenient **NOTEBOOK** at the end of this edition.
Whether on vacation, travelling or at home, you can easily organize your new knowledge without needing a second notebook!

5) FINISHED?

Go to the bonus section: **MONSTER CHALLENGE** to find a free game offered at the end of this edition!

Want more fun and learning activities? It's **Fast and Simple!**
An entire Game Book Collection just **one click away!**

Find your next challenge at:

BestActivityBooks.com/MyNextWordSearch

Ready, Set... Go!

Did you know there are around 7,000 different languages in the world? Words are precious.

We love languages and have been working hard to make the highest quality books for you. Our ingredients?

A selection of indispensable learning themes, three big slices of fun, then we add a spoonful of difficult words and a pinch of rare ones. We serve them up with care and a maximum of delight so you can solve the best word games and have fun learning!

Your feedback is essential. You can be an active participant in the success of this book by leaving us a review. Tell us what you liked most in this edition!

Here is a short link which will take you to your order page.

BestBooksActivity.com/Review50

Thanks for your help and enjoy the Game!

Linguas Classics Team

1 - Antiques

```
L  T  T  D  T  L  M  K  K  H  R  Q  O  R
P  S  S  G  H  I  E  O  H  I  W  O  S  J
E  E  A  N  E  L  N  S  K  A  V  C  I  G
T  L  O  V  K  E  M  I  M  H  B  O  Š  O
E  I  A  A  I  M  P  B  B  L  O  A  T  S
T  S  O  L  S  O  V  A  E  E  S  A  N  T
S  O  S  U  O  K  E  H  T  K  T  M  A  E
O  B  T  E  U  G  L  K  F  H  E  O  O  L
S  C  E  X  I  M  E  O  W  O  L  E  Š  E
E  B  S  L  N  X  L  M  J  L  E  K  T  S
M  A  K  H  A  B  A  N  E  H  B  E  I  U
F  O  D  K  R  H  H  Q  L  O  E  T  L  P
V  S  Y  X  H  D  K  L  E  O  Š  S  N  T
L  I  T  S  E  L  I  S  O  A  T  I  F  I
```

LITŠOANTŠISO	PETETSO
THEKISO	MAKHABANE
TŠEBELETSO	KHALE
LEKHOLHOOA	THEKO
LITS'ELISO	KHABANE
MOEKETSI	PUSELETSO
LILEMO	SETS'OAOA
MOKHABISO	MOKHOA
TS'ELISO	VALUE
KHALELE	

2 - Food #1

```
K M F C Q P E R E S E B E L
I P A K A B I H T C Z M Z U
N K K B K P H F E P F R O M
A U S O O W V U O M F R H A
M N E T N L O P H T U N A N
O U G E R O I H E X R L R Y
X M A L H A F L S Z M E S A
B A S E L A W O A T B K S N
B L S L E N C B L N V O A E
A I O E T H G K E E E A L S
L R P B A D Q Z C R T N A E
A I O E M A S E K O R E T S
L S S S L E T S W A I Y E Q
I D R T S E P I N I C H I B
```

MABOLILANE	LEKOANE
BALALI	PERE
BASELA	SALATE
SEHOETE	LETSWAI
KINAMO	SOPO
KONOFOLE	SEPINICHI
MASEKO	STRAWBERRY
SIRILAMUNU	TS'EBELE
LEBESE	TUNA
ANYANESE	THIBAKA

3 - Measurements

```
T L G N L I T E R E J O A O
Y M G I L A M I C E D X S H
R B B A E E K I L O M E L A
O M U L O B K I M X A B U O
N B O T E B O O N V R E I C
C M Y V N E Q B L C G L E E
E E M Z Q A W P Y O H E Q N
T H O L O A N A X T U L G T
Q T K L X A T P M Y E E M I
P Q H I P L B J A S I S A M
L L F H I A N A N O T L Y E
M O T S O T S O O C C X R R
K I L O M E T E R E Q L E E
B B O L E M O B O H L A L E
```

BYTE	BELELE
CENTIMERE	LITERE
DECIMALI	MASISA
LEKOLO	METALA
BOTEBO	MOTSOTSO
GRAM	ONCE
BOLEMO	TONANA
INCH	BOLUMO
KILOMELA	THOLOANA
KILOMETERE	BOHLALE

4 - Farm #2

```
L J R R E E M F R L E B L T
G W N Z A N A O L O H T I E
J W N Y A A K S L F J U J B
D R L T F Y A Q E E R X O I
O J Y W O N F S V N M H D R
L L A M A U E M P A B I H I
B R V E H K S J O T O R O M
P D Z G B I R M M L S Q K K
Q H D W F L U C T O I O U H
L I P H O O F O L O L S L O
Q J B A L A L I P C E I A L
N K U L E T A T A A S R K O
L E B E S E N O O P T J X O
B U L U T S E N G E J C U F
```

LIPHOOFOLO	LLAMA
BALALI	LEBESE
MOLIKO	SEFAKA
POONE	BULUTSENG
LETATA	LIKUNYANE
MOLEMI	MOLISA
LIJO	TEBIRI
THOLOANA	MOROTO
TS'ELISO	KHOLO
NKU	

5 - Books

```
L E Q E P H E I L O G N O M
T L O G G I S T E K E O M Y
T Š B J X I X G B A B B P C
S T E L E B O N O O I P A O
O L N B F H A O K O L H E L
A H A M E V Q T O R L A K E
N O B O P L Q H R P F S H M
E K A L P O E L K A M T O U
L O H E F L T T Q L A E L T
O M K L Y O E S S E N B O I
T E O E X K G P O O T E A O
G L O K T O E Q I A S L D B
Z O P I R B D C W C O L E Y
I B O H L O K O L J E O H S
```

BOITUMELO	LEQEPHE
MONGOLI	LEBOKO
BOKOLO	POTSO
TEBELLO	MOEKETSI
KHABANE	TLHOKOMELO
EPIC	LEHLOKOA
TS'OANELO	PALE
TŠEBELETSO	BOHLOKO
MOLELEKI	MANTSOE
NOBELE	KHOLOA

6 - Meditation

```
M  M  I  N  O  N  P  A  S  B  M  T  J  L
T  Q  B  G  V  G  B  O  Q  Q  O  L  P  I
O  L  L  E  B  E  T  S  K  E  T  H  H  K
Y  G  H  T  H  A  B  O  H  N  S  O  E  E
T  S  B  A  H  V  D  S  O  E  A  K  F  L
I  E  Y  I  H  T  F  T  T  H  M  O  O  E
I  S  G  R  H  O  S  S  E  A  M  L  T
K  A  M  O  H  E  L  O  O  L  I  E  L  S
Z  M  O  L  B  M  Z  S  R  O  K  L  E  O
Y  Q  O  H  O  B  E  T  W  B  Z  O  L  D
B  N  G  S  K  G  V  E  E  G  X  Y  E  A
Q  X  V  I  A  E  H  I  S  D  H  V  K  O
O  S  O  S  T  A  M  S  U  Q  E  M  O  I
E  F  A  G  R  O  S  T  O  P  O  N  O  P
```

KAMOHELO	MOSA
TSOSOA	KELELLO
PHEFO	MOTSAMAI
TSIETSO	MMINO
TLHOKOMELO	TLHAHO
QENEHELO	TEBELLO
MATSOSO	PONO POTSO
TEBOHO	KHOTSO
MEKHOA	LIKELETSO
THABO	

7 - Days and Months

```
K P Q Y E N A J T P U H P P
Y C N V E A N P P P K S Z H
E B J G T E B K R E U E D A
X A D D J Q A H B I Y L L K
I S K L C L Y A M M L E G A
M O S O T H O B P D S M A N
B E K E T S O A W V J O O E
O I L C T K E N A O K E H P
A L O K A L H E O E Y J K G
H K H A L E N D A T D L G E
T S E L I S O L E N A O Š T
E L T Š E P A N E J O H C M
H K H O E L I J P X Z E P U
K M O Q E H L O F Y Z F P M
```

APRIL	KHOELI
PHAKANE	TŠOANELO
KHALENDA	MPHATO
HLAKOLA	MOQEHLO
KHETHA	TŠEPANE
PHEKOANE	KHABANE
PHUPTJANE	TS'ELISO
MAY	BEKETSO
MOSOTHO	SELEMO

8 - Energy

```
D U M M O T S A M A I D M L
K H E T H I S O F E H P H E
K M A F U R A X F A E S J T
M H M L E B E T H A H C W S
O C A E S O K O N Z P B M A
C N E B J N O R T C E L E T
H P T E A N I L O S A G S
E Z S E B N S K U E H E T I
S N O S I L E S T R Q P S O
O M Y Z M O T L A T S I O V
T I K O L O H O L T Z F A O
T Š I L A F A L O Z R R N M
I N D A K A N E W A F Z E A
V B E X M O E K E T S I S Z
```

LEBETHA	MOCHESO
KHABANE	MOEKETSI
TS'ELISO	INDAKANE
MOTLATSI	NOKOSEA
ELECTRON	PHOTO
TS'OANE	TŠILAFALO
KHETHISO	STEAM
TIKOLOHO	LETSATSI
MAFURA	MOTSAMAI
GASOLINE	PHEFO

9 - Archeology

```
W C I E R A P C L V K T L S
E L A H K E L A H K O M E E
L F M M M O P A S A M S B M
I F A O S C N X L L U U I P
E T S E Q N A J L H N N T H
K S T K L I L E M O O Y L I
E E O E T S E B A N G M A R
T L M T R L I E K E T S O I
S I F S G E S E T S E B I G
A S N I W K L T E A M B H P
N O B E O S T E O S T C X H
A K J F W P B I K Q R V S S
N T E M P E L E H V N Q T B
L E B E L A N G Z I W Y E F
```

TS'ELISO
MOKHALE-KHALE
MASAPO
TS'OETSOE
ERA
SETSEBI
LEBELANG
MOHLALA
LIEKETSANA
SEMPHIRI

LIEKETSO
MOTSAMAI
RELEK
MOEKETSI
TEAM
TEMPELE
LEBITLA
TSEBANG
LILEMO

10 - Food #2

```
S  M  V  S  H  E  M  O  R  A  O  M  B  N
W  Y  T  Q  D  L  L  U  Q  R  Q  U  F  M
U  L  E  R  I  T  A  M  A  T  S  S  J  L
T  S  E  L  I  S  O  B  C  I  B  H  J  I
S  B  K  K  H  O  H  O  H  C  A  R  U  H
O  E  R  I  X  G  I  U  E  H  N  O  W  L
O  S  L  O  W  E  F  J  S  O  A  O  Z  A
J  I  O  E  C  I  A  X  E  K  N  M  A  P
E  A  P  U  R  C  R  B  V  E  A  K  P  I
J  R  G  M  H  I  O  T  P  C  S  H  O  N
L  E  H  E  Y  W  M  L  Z  H  P  O  L  M
E  G  G  P  L  A  N  T  I  E  F  L  E  X
Y  O  K  O  T  E  K  W  U  R  X  O  Y  S
I  I  T  X  X  V  H  E  H  I  J  N  I  E
```

APOLE	EGGPLANT
ARTICHOKE	LIHLAPI
BANANA	MORAFI
BROCCOLI	HEMO
SELERI	KIWI
CHESE	MUSHROOM
CHERI	RAISE
KHOHO	TAMATI
TS'ELISO	KHOLO
LEHE	YOKOTE

11 - Chemistry

```
D M F S R E N P P I X I O Q
B N O R T C E L E S A H K A
Z O C C L M S N Y T A M S L
Q H O V H L I T Š E P E E K
X A H S U E A F K Q V N N A
M P C V L T S O M O T A S L
O E L I P P J O B M Y B E I
L S T E D E N N Y M E A H N
E T S C T G X Y J I G H F E
K X E I E S P V V O Q K P K
H B L H D R W B V N T Q D E
U A I E P F F A E S O K O N
E H S H G B E N I R O L H C
S B O I M O E K E T S I O O
```

ACID
ALKALINE
ATOMO
KHABANE
TS'ELISO
CHLORINE
ELECTRON
ENNYME
KHASE
MOCHESO

MOEKETSI
ION
MOQETSI
LITŠEPE
MOLEK'HUE
NOKOSEA
TS'EPA
OKSENSE
LETSWAI

12 - Music

```
Q Y M Y D H B I E C D A M S
T T V X M A M A P X C J A E
R E R L H R J I L D M A I B
M E T S A M F T N A V Y K E
T O S U R O H C C O L E R L
L S T S E N H P K H P A O I
A T A H P I L E P O M I O S
K E L P O C I T C E L E F A
O L B H S M L I M S P J A L
A E U E I D O L E M K G N W
U B M L T B A T C P X K E K
N E X A E D L T H J R Z Y D
I Š T T O X O R L O E N J Z
R T T M P M M T S E L I S O
```

ALBUM
BALALA
CHORUS
ELECTIC
HARMONIC
TS'ELISO
SEBELISA
MOLAOLI
MELODI

MAIKROOFANE
MINOPI
OPERA
POETISO
TLAKOA
MOTHO MOTHO
TŠEBELETSOE
PHELA
MOPELI

13 - Family

```
K M M O T S E O A C M S B Z
A H A E V F S A N A O S T X
N A A T U F X Z A B K A B M
N G Y S S L K A B A H C O M
T T O D A O L O S T A N N M
L S L A N N A E L M B T M O
O X O G N P E N K T A A O S
A P H M O A N A E I N T H A
N Y O O M W A O S O E E L L
A N L T I M Y S I U P A A I
R V T S Q V N T M O Y F K X
A Z N E I L O L T N B G A B
Q Z Y L F K M V G O C T N N
T S H I M O T S O A L I E G
```

NTLOLI
MOHLAKANE
MOKHABANE
NGOANA
TS'OANA
BANA
TS'OANE
NTATE
NTLOANA
NTLOHOLO

TS'OLO
MONNA
MOTS'ELI
MOTS'EOA
MOCHABA
MONYANE
MOTSOALI
KHASANE
MATS'OANE
MOSALI

14 - Farm #1

```
M H A Y G A M U Z X B H V T
O N A M A N A N E P E O E M
K B M Q F F T W S Y G M K C
H L I Z W S Š K I T R E H T
O Y E S T C O A A T G T O Š
O W S T O E A T R E K S M E
K C E W Š N N S C M S I O N
O L A J D A E E B O B X K Y
A U E G K T B Z N N T J A A
M E L K A L W O K H O H O N
B J I T H P H I R I U H S E
B S M C R O M O N O A N E U
X D U N C U T P H O K O D I
W X W H V L D A Y O Y D J S
```

TEMO
BEE
BISON
NAMANANE
KATSE
KHOHO
KHOMO
MOKHOOKOA
NTJA
TŠOANE

LEKHOTA
MONOANE
LETŠABO
PHOKODI
HAY
TŠENYANE
PHIRI
RAISE
PEO
METSI

15 - Camping

```
T O B A P T K K A N O E W Y
E T A F I L S O D G H F A P
N R K G I A O O P A H T K F
T M O L L O V R M A O O H K
E H Q S E K O P I I S L L H
N I Q S N M L L L W B E E A
G Z G D A A O Y E N I M T M
H M N K B P F T O F M U Š M
I U E C A Q O W H T M T E O
D H B X H T O C K J F I T K
U F A P K A H D F C Y O Š O
M E H L A R P U L Q V B E S
V T T Z J W I T L H A H O F
U W Z G N E L E B A H T D P
```

BOITUMELO
LIPHOOFOLO
KHABANE
KANOE
KOPASE
MOLLO
MEHLA
THABELENG
HAMMOKO
SEKOPI

TSOMI
KHOOA
LETŠETŠE
MAP
KHOELI
THABENG
TLHAHO
THAPO
TENTENG
LIFATE

16 - Algebra

```
Z E R O D K Q Q M L F N B F
K A R O H A N O I W B B V O
T M T W Z N U V M X F V J W
F Š O S X X K D O H T E Z Y
E T E T E S G O L E B A H T
T Q S B S L V K H A B A N E
O J V R E A I M O L Z L M T
H O N G V L M S M E B O A S
A O H K O M E A O M O K T O
L E S H A N O T I O T A R A
M O E K E T S I S K H L I N
M O T S E L I S I O A H X E
K E R A F A Y G Q L T O B L
N U M B E R Q F K H A M R O
```

TŠEBELETSO   MOKHOA
KAROHANO   MATRIX
KHABANE   NUMBER
MOHLAKOLA   MOTS'ELISI
TS'OANELO   BOTHATA
LESHANO   HLOKOMELA
MOTSAMAI   THABELO
MOEKETSI   TS'ELISO
KERAFA   FETOHA
MOHLOMI   ZERO

17 - Spices

```
K O R I A N D E C V L P Q S
T H Y A R S O T U A E A J T
T L B W A Z C E M N T P Y V
H L N S H W V R I I S R B L
A H U T K M J A N L O I O L
M D T E B N O K H A A K H I
A K M L E U M N K I N A L K
N J E G S Z U Z A I E I O O
A F G R E T F B T T N B K P
J E K I N O R F A S E A O O
F N S O A M H J M E M Z M X
E N B I Y L E L A J Z Q D O
L E N M N F R X N A I Y G H
E L B Q A A E L O F O N O K
```

ANISE	KONOFOLE
BOHLOKO	THAMANA
KARETE	LIKOPO
KINAMO	NUTMEG
LETS'OANE	ANYANESE
KORIANDE	PAPRIKA
CUMIN	SAFRONIKE
KHARA	LETSWAI
FENNEL	MONATE
TAMANO	VANILA

18 - Universe

```
E O P O K E S E L E H T X L
N Y H H A A L E S T K R U E
A S T E R O I D B E K D O B
Y E N A B A H K W A K M I O
N Q T L E F I F I U K O D K
A U S K K H O T S O B A P O
K A O Y H S S E B A Q L A I
N T A I C A I D O Z S A X D
A O N S N E L E L A L H K L
L R E W C Q E A U T L A H U
H J L G N V S Z X U E N O K
O E O H J K T N R E L O E S
M L E H O L I M O H H B L V
T L H O K O M E L I S O I A
```

ASTEROID
MOHLANKANYANE
TS'OANELO
SEBAKA
LEHOLIMO
KHOTSO
LEFIFI
EQUATOR
KHALAXE
KHABANE

TS'ELISO
LEBOKO
KHOELI
TSELA
SEKOPI
HLALELE
TLHOKOMELISO
THELESEKOPO
BONAHALA
ZODIAC

19 - Mammals

```
K A N G A R O O G X Z W O K
E R N G I M O W M O I P L A
H B Y A D I O U H X R K O T
Y E E O Y V S T E J I I D S
H Z D V W N B E Š K H H L E
T A U A V M A F A O P Q O A
T L O T L O L L S J E F U C
D O L P H I N X T V G N X R
P H O K O J O E E U X T E Q
B W Y S H M K R B S M B O F
F R N K O Y O T E L E B E B
H C T U P W H O L H U H T I
H D J M O H L A K O L A K A
N I A K A M E L A G I X P U
```

BEBELE
LEBETSA
POHO
KAMELA
KATSE
KOYOTE
NTJA
DOLPHIN
TLOTLO
PHOKOJOE

THUHLO
GORILA
KANGAROO
TAUA
MOTŠOENE
MUTLANYANA
MOHLAKOLA
PHIRI
ZEBRA

20 - Fishing

```
L L W V H P A N A O L O H T
I E P E K E S B C W C P L L
E B O B Z L I W A I O H E J
K O L B S E L T G I H E O Z
E T L D E H E O O S T H E J
T E E L X P B P P T C E T S
S N M W E A E A O E I T L S
E G E U Q M S L H M L S E J
N B T B E A A O K E S A Z Q
G H E T N B J M E H S H S P
N O H M N E L E T Š E T Š E
C S P M O H L A H A R E U X
B A S E K A H O K A N E P D
R I G S R N X U M J L U M U
```

BAIT
BASEKA
LEBOTENG
SEKEPE
PHEHETSA
SEBELISA
PHETEMELLO
MAPHELE
LIEKETSENG
HOKANE

MOHLAHARE
LETŠETŠE
LEOETLE
MAMELLO
MOLAPO
SEKOA
METSI
THOLOANA
KHOPO

21 - Restaurant #1

```
L M W L O F W Q B O H O B E
L I O N I P O K E S R S R K
P D E K I J S K E E G I B O
R T I K H A O K A N I L X F
S Q O H E E S Z Z I S E M I
W A P I H T T Z R K T M O F
M A H F O P S H Z P E O T M
G U U V W Z L E I A I K S W
J P E K E T S O N N S O E M
L E T S E L I S I G T H L E
E O R N O R Z D Q U T L I N
N P U G S K T O H H R T S U
C P B Q C T E O E T E S I F
K H O H O K H O M A X M E V
```

TLHOKOMELISO   TSIETSI
SEKOPI   THIPA
BOHOBE   KHOMA
MOKHETHI   MENU
KHOHO   NAPKIN
KOFI   PEKETSO
LETS'ELISI   SOSO
LIJO   LINAKO
LIEKETSENG   MOTS'ELISI

22 - Bees

```
L M M D I S T A S T E L T F
T I P O J I L I H S N K Š A
S H P O F F O H S E T H E P
E V R A L U U S H L Š A N A
P V H A L E M I L I E B Y N
O N M E J E L A W S P I A E
F B W B D Q S M H O A T N N
H L A B A N E A K A K A E G
P O L L I N A T O R L U Z V
T H O L O A N A W F W I E G
M O L E M O Q Y M O S I O E
R B V F S O V H I V E Z Q G
R G B E O H F I C K U K C I
P N M N V K G J Q S U A D N
```

MOLEMO
TS'ELISO
FAPANENG
TS'EPO
LIPALESA
LIJO
THOLOANA
TŠEPA
KHABITA
HIVE

TŠENYANE
KHOOA
LIMELA
MPOLE
POLLINATOR
MOFUMAHALI
MOSIO
LETSATSI
HLABANE
KAKA

23 - Weather

```
M F B M K F Q Y F Q X I S X
O O R O P O H T O S E L I B
T G V H D L M P C V Y E O K
L A P L Z E I E O M E T S A
A N O O P T A N L L L V T L
T E L M H S N K E O U F E E
S J A I E O F E F E S R L R
I I R P F A M U D A E S E U
A X L D O N U Q Q A Q V B U
W W O S T E I S T K C I E A
L U S E H L O K O A N E Š Q
M O L E M O T S I B J U T H
S E K O P I L E Q E T S A R
E N H L U I A M A S T O M G
```

SEBAKA	MOTLATSI
MOTSAMAI	MOHLOMI
TSIETSO	POLAR
LESOTHO	MOLEMOTSI
LERUU	SEKOPI
KOMELO	SEFEFO
OMETSA	SEADUMA
FOGANE	SEHLOKOANE
LETS'OANE	TŠEBELETSO
LEQETSA	PHEFO

24 - Adventure

```
W C I A Z U R W K T X M P C
Z I S E B E T E M G A O H H
Y H U L K U C J G C H N A E
M A E T O J W W C J T Y K S
M K W N E T H A B O S E I E
A A P O L O K O T S E T S H
T B E B L S R Q L T L L O O
H E A V A T A F H A I A S K
A L F G O E Z O A K S Z S M
T H Y H S I Y U H A O Y F N
A S C J T S W C O M L J C D
W K E O O T S E B E T S O Q
X I T L M M O S E B E T S I
T L O A E L E H A N G N D F
```

MOSEBETSI
BONTLE
SEBETE
MATHATA
MONYETLA
TSIETSO
LEBAKA
CHESEHO
TS'ELISO
MOTSOALLE

TS'EBETSO
THABO
TLHAHO
MOCHA
PHAKISO
POLOKO
MAKATSO
MAETO
TLOAELEHANG

25 - Sport

```
H M K L M X F F J R F H S M
A H Z H R O S E J H E M M O
L E T O I L A P A P I L O T
P M O S K L B T V V E C T S
K M M T P E I O H F G R B A
V E A E O M S W K I D E O M
H L S L O A T X S H B G L A
M E I E U M E B A L O E I I
A M R B A E K E L A P P L R
S A I E U O E N A N E L O I
A T M Š H J O I N J H J I P
P L C T C U M Q T O P P Q E
O A V G C H D P H O L O S O
G S E P H E O A I S O K B U
```

BOKHOPO
MOATHIBELI
MMELE
MASAPO
BAEKELA
MOTSAMAI
JESO
MAMELLO
SEPHEO

PHOLOSO
TŠEBELETSO
MOEKETSI
MOTBOLI
MASIRI
PHEPO
LENANEO
LIPAPALI
MATLA

26 - Circus

```
T I G E R E L G G U J Z T P
M E R N M O T Š O E N E L A
L O C I E F C P F N K F O R
I R L K D T D W N A H B T A
P A X O E V N S U O O O L D
H M A P I T K E D L T H O E
O L U L O K M H T O S L R U
O B A C N V M Q C B O O A M
F G T Š P L I F Q I R K P O
O G C J T E N L U L D O A B
L U E O C N O I I I T A E E
O E X R Z C O S J R V V S L
N T L I G N A B A H T V D I
A C R O B A T M O N A T E I
```

ACROBAT	BOHLOKOA
LIPHOOFOLO	MOLOI
LIBOLOANE	MOTŠOENE
MONATE	MMINO
KOLULO	PARADE
SEAPARO	BONTŠA
TLOTLO	MOBELI
THABANG	TENTENG
JUGGLER	TIGER
TAUA	KHOTSO

27 - Restaurant #2

```
L V O J X T E D D C I U E M
L I A W S T E L A W V Q X E
I I M G F B T W S O Y R H T
R Z H A Q W O S T O R E M S
C M F L N R F A E K K T K I
I O S R A E I L Q N R Š H M
S M O D N P Z A E I M E A O
G V P U A Z I T L L J B B T
M I O D O Y Z E K E K E A H
B A D E L G U Y S P T L N U
Z F H U O H L K N H C E E S
B O K E H O S I L E S T Q I
S Y O Q T R S N T K X S Z R
T H A B E L E N G O M O X G
```

KEKE	LIMANE
TS'ELISO	SALATE
THABELENG	LETSWAI
TŠEBELETSO	SOPO
MAHE	LINKO
LIHLAPI	KHABANE
PHEKO	MEROTSO
THOLOANA	MOTHUSI
LEQETSA	METSI

28 - Geology

```
W W O N A C L O V Q V O Z L
L E B A T L A I Y T A R G I
I S F Q E G Y K T S O M L T
Z T R A U Q R H Z Š H S J S
T A D I C A L A L H O M N E
Š L V H B B F B K O H E B P
I A R A G Y T A O D O F L A
S C Z Y L Y P N R V H T W E
I T L E J W E E A T K K N L
N I A W S T E L L C E M S E
Y T K O X R R R E S Y E G R
E E U Z K L E H A K A K X A
H Y S B I O K A L A T Š I S
O L I E K E T S E N G Q Z A
```

ACID	GEYSER
KALATŠI	LAVA
LEHAKA	LERASA
KHABANE	LITS'EPA
KORALE	LEBATLA
LITŠOELE	QUARTZ
LIEKETSENG	LETSWAI
TŠISINYEHO	STALACTITE
KHOHOHOA	LEJWE
MOHLALA	VOLCANO

29 - House

```
A K A R A R E T E T C E R C
T S I E T S I D S N B Z D X
S E N A O S T I L E K S P A
L I K E K E T S O E L H T B
A W S Y A P E Š T N B I J R
K U B Q Y D A M G O H A S J
L E B O N A T N M B S C K O
L F C G O U T Y U E F Y Z A
F E A E M I I Q Z S M K S Z
L R K D A L C A H L A T S A
R O Z H M O E K E T S I V K
P M P U O L E F I E L E G T
Z A F P Q T L E B O T A S K
M K T U N O A R U F A R Z C
```

ATTIC	LITS'OANE
LEFIELE	TSIETSI
LIKEKETSO	LEBONA
MONYAKO	MOEKETSI
LEKHOTA	SEBONE
LEBAKA	RAFURA
TS'ELISO	KAMORE
KARARE	HLATS'A
TŠEPA	LEBOTA

30 - Physics

```
T G Q T W V Y E L S Z E K P
A S I S A M C U M X Y O H H
G T W R W U R H R B B S E A
N W O L E M O K O H L T M T
E X O M S O A E L K T E I L
S R K J Q Z Q L E A S R K A
T Š O A N E L O B M O A H L
E Z S M O T S M E A A K A A
K K T W R E X A L N N A L T
E H E Q T N L O H O E P E S
I L K F C A E S O K O N U O
L G E X E K M O T S A M A I
C P K U L A V E L O C I T Y
H E C M E M S E H L O O H O
```

PHATLALATSO	MAKANETE
ATOM	MASISA
TLHOKOMELO	LIEKETSENG
K'HEMIK'HALE	MOLEK'HUE
TŠOANELO	NOKOSEA
ELECTRON	SEHLOOHO
TS'OANE	KAMANO
MOTSAMAI	LEBELO
KEKETSO	PAKARETSO
KHASE	VELOCITY

31 - Colors

```
L C U Z G L M P Q E M D M W
Y J S C B T O H U H O Z T Z
V I O L E T P E W A N A Y C
N S E P I A U P J G A T J V
K A K N I P T H P J H N M W
T J M M A N S I F N A E L B
Š N A U I O R C K N G X E
O J W A N Q Š I A G A A A I
E F R G Z U A T R X R M O G
U M G J Q U B O T S O O A E
T Š E H L A R F U C H S I A
N B Y V D O B E H Q K S F D
K H I B I D U D U A K N M Y
O U X P U T S O A I I C A H
```

AZURE
BEIGE
TŠOANE
PUTSOA
BOTSOOA
CYAN
FUCHSIA
MONAHANA
MOPUTSO

MAGENTA
NAMUNU
PINK
PHEPHIRI
KHIBIDUDU
SEPIA
VIOLET
TŠOEU
TŠEHLA

32 - Shapes

```
L A V O S I L E S T B Z P M
G E B U C M S I R P L I Y O
E O H C L H O L S A D W R T
L L T L C N W K C R G L A S
E H L V A B B X H C M E M A
O F D I Q K G N J O I K I M
Š H U S P Y O Y O Y A A D A
T S E S I S N A O N E K G I
A K A B E S E E N A B A H K
M P O L Y O N E K A D R C W
R S E K O N A I I M Y E C L
U O X J E P X K O N A N O E
M O H O L O O A V Y U V R R
X Z W J H G P R G Q O J L N
```

ARC	OVAL
KONA	POLYONE
SEK'ONA	PRISM
CUBE	PYRAMID
MOTSAMAI	KHABANE
MATŠOELE	LEHLAKOANA
ELLIPSE	SEBAKA
MOHOLO OA	LEKAKARE
MOKHOA	TS'ELISO

33 - Scientific Disciplines

```
K H E M I T H I B K M E L B
L I R O B O T O F O I G I O
T Š O O L O W Z N K N E E E
P H I R I L O E K H E O K M
T S E P O T Š E P O R L E O
T Š E B E L E T S O A O T H
M T M L X M B K F P L J S O
O S O G I A D J I E O I E L
T E T M R P R C H H G K N O
S H A Z Z Z U T L P O A G D
O L N Y Y P P O A J G C G M
A O A B O T A N Y A N E P H
O K K I N E S I O L O J I L
A O L E N A O S T O Z A Z G
```

ANATOME
TŠEPO
TS'OANELO
TS'EPO
BOTANYANE
KHEMITHI
GEOLOJI
MOTS'OAOA
KINESIOLOJI
LIPUO

LIEKETSENG
BOEMOHOLO
MINERALOGO
PHEPO
FIHLA
PHIRILOE
TS'EHLOKO
LIROBOTO
TŠEBELETSO
TŠOOLO

34 - Science

```
I S Q E L A H K I M E H K D
L Q J A L E M I L B T F Z A
E A H U S J K E Z T C M T T
H P B K E N A E S T O M L A
O E A O H K O M L V K A H Z
H S H M R B V L V E C P A F
K T F F T A A O H O T E H P
J I O I P X T J D N E S O M
U L H E H R X O A W L T O O
K A T O M L Q N R T E M H H
J N O F W T A O H I B W F L
X J S L I E K E T S E N G A
A D E U H K E L O M S A D L
N O L L E B E T A A I O T A
```

ATOM
K'HEMIK'HALE
LESOTHO
DATA
PHETOHOA
LEKELETSO
SEBELE
MOHLALA
KHOHELI
LABORATORI

MOKHOA
LITS'EPA
MOLEK'HUE
TLHAHO
TEBELLO
TS'EPA
LIEKETSENG
FIHLA
LIMELA
MOTS'EANE

35 - Beauty

```
B  S  P  H  O  T  O  G  E  N  I  C  J  P
A  H  G  I  M  A  K  O  L  O  A  N  E  L
E  A  M  A  S  C  A  R  A  R  C  I  Y  E
M  M  B  O  E  L  A  N  A  U  F  Y  Q  T
L  P  D  L  K  O  S  I  H  A  L  H  I  L
I  O  S  T  E  L  E  B  E  Š  T  I  L  A
K  O  M  O  H  A  U  M  I  B  L  H  O  L
H  L  I  K  H  A  L  A  A  H  I  W  A  O
O  S  K  H  A  B  A  N  E  O  L  S  L  S
P  K  H  A  H  L  I  S  O  W  L  G  O  E
O  T  S  E  L  I  S  O  Z  H  M  I  M  B
L  I  P  S  T  I  M  O  L  E  M  O  Q  O
M  O  K  H  A  K  O  N  E  H  U  I  Y  N
S  E  K  E  L  E  S  I  S  R  Q  K  P  E
```

KHAHLISO	SEBONE
MOLAOLI	MAOLI
LIKHOPO	PHOTOGENIC
LIKHALA	LIHLAHISO
KHABANE	MAKOLOANE
MOKHAKO	SEKELESI
MOHAU	LITŠEBELETSO
LIPSTI MOLEMO	SHAMPOO
BOELANA	LETLALO
MASCARA	TS'ELISO

36 - Clothes

```
G J T Y A Q M Y H N T M L S
N L W I O Z E O L F N A P E
V S E E T E T W L M Y K U N
B L O U S E T E K A J H T J
L S E B A K A E R A K A S R
S I T O K E S N I O X B O F
J O H X H Q N Q X H C A E G
A E O L E N A O S T T N W C
T P A T A L T A B E L E S E
U E I N Q B M O A P A R O H
F H L H E S A M A J A P A R
E S H W W P Y N O R P A K X
S E B A K E L O E P B B L S
L I T Š O A N E S E K O P I
```

APRON	JEANE
LEBATLA	MAKHABANE
BLOUSE	PAJAMAS
SEBAKA	PUTSOE
SEBAKELO	LIHLABANE
MOAPARO	SAKARE
TS'OANELO	SHEPE
LITŠOANE	SEETE
SEKOPI	SEKOTI
JAKETE	SEFUTA

37 - Insects

```
I  T  D  C  P  E  O  G  H  G  C  A  Q  M
L  F  E  I  B  S  S  Y  Y  L  U  U  C  A
M  D  O  A  U  E  T  E  K  K  O  J  U  N
T  W  L  D  F  B  E  N  A  B  O  H  K  T
R  Š  H  A  O  A  R  M  O  T  S  O  A  I
U  X  E  X  H  K  M  L  H  U  E  W  V  S
F  G  O  B  K  A  I  E  T  L  R  Y  R  E
I  F  L  I  E  H  T  T  O  H  R  D  A  R
J  E  H  I  L  L  E  S  M  V  C  B  L  D
B  K  E  W  Y  R  E  A  Y  W  J  X  Z  S
N  E  L  Y  G  V  V  T  E  X  A  J  T  N
K  A  E  Z  Q  R  Z  S  J  Q  U  S  X  A
L  E  T  S  I  E  D  I  H  P  A  Z  P  A
R  V  I  P  E  R  S  E  B  O  K  A  J  W
```

NTJA	LEHLOEHLOE
APHID	LARVA
BEE	LETSIE
KHOBANE	MANTISE
SEBAKA	MOTS'OA
CIADA	MOTHO
LEKHOFU	TERMITE
TŠEBELE	WASP
LETSATSI	SEBOKA

38 - Astronomy

```
T E B E L L O R R B W Y R C
S A T E L L I T E O B W B P
N E B U L A L D L Q K D E Z
X O O L N C A I D O Z E S E
R U V U M C O P A L O M T R
K H A L A X E S P A T W P E
M A H L A T S I M V W M L Š
E K T S E L I S O O Y O A T
L Q P R A U L O U N S T N A
E K U K Y S E S P R U S E F
L X Q I J Y O M V E S A T E
A F A Y N U H P W P H M E L
L S J I P O K E S U W A F M
H F N R N Q X K I S Q I W Q
```

MOTSAMAI	TEBELLO
TS'ELISO	PLANETE
COSMOS	MAHLATSI
LEFATŠE	ROKETE
EQUINOX	SATELLITE
KHALAXE	SEKOPI
MOLAPO	HLALELE
KHOELI	SUPERNOVA
NEBULA	ZODIAC

39 - Health and Wellness #2

```
D L I T Š O A N T Š I S O I
K H A T H A T S O I U L W B
V R G B I K A L O R I X A G
O C L M S O K J S E C O K M
S E P E E L E L I H P E H P
T V M M K H R O L D P J G B
E I M O A M C M E A H E J O
L T O O T T A V S J E S U H
E A K T L A L A T W P O A L
B M H W Y B N A S G O T K O
E I O S M U C A L A B O R K
Š N A T L F M A S I S A T O
T X O L B E Q X N D E F J T
J A A Y E L T H O L O A N A
```

ANATOME
MALI
KALORI
JESO
LEFUBA
MATLA
LITŠOANTŠISO
PHEPHILE
SEPEELE
BOHLOKO

TŠEBELETSO
MASISA
MOKHOAOA
PHEPO
TS'ELISO
ROBALA
KHATHATSO
VITAMIN
THOLOANA

40 - Time

```
B E K E T S O S U D D A Q H
T S O A N E L O I U A E B A
F S D G T L F X S S J E R U
M E L E B Š T O M M H X F
P L O D G P H U B Y P G N I
E E M L E K H O L H O O A N
W M O S O M A K O B K J L Y
T O S K H A L E N D A N E A
K S O M O T S O T S O H T N
R H O H O N A J O A L E S E
A R O H M A O B A N E W A X
V S J E L K Z G U E J J T N
A E P S L E L E B Š T S G
I J T Y N I G O G O S J I P
```

PELE
KHALENDA
LEKHOLHOOA
TŠEBELE
LETSATSI
SELEMO
TSOHLE
BOKAMOSO
HORA
MOTSOTSO

KHOELI
MOSO
BOSIU
MOTŠEBELE
HONA JOALE
HAUFINYANE
TS'OANELO
BEKETSO
MAOBANE

41 - Buildings

```
K K J N Z U P X M Q R Y M B
H H J B T V C S W O Y M X W
O M A H O L T B D X L U N A
S P P H L O O K E H P I P W
T G J Y L X G A S T S D K Y
E L Z H E I B Z S Y B A J O
L D J O B V S Q J A F T Y M
E H O T E L E O Y U R S G U
X T O S T E L E B E Š T V S
U K A R A R E N A B A H K E
S Y E T E N T E N G V T I M
S E K O L O P O L A S I F O
S U P A M A K E T E C U A T
M O K H A B A N E L C Q D W
```

PHEKO
MOLIKO
KHABANE
KHAHLISO
NTLOASA
MOKHABANE
POLASI
KARARE
HOSTELE

HOTELE
MUSEMO
SEKOLO
STADIUM
SUPAMAKETE
TENTENG
TŠEBELETSO
TEBELLO

42 - Gardening

```
P Y L A S E L A P I L J B D
L E S O H E F U W F V Q R I
E W O D D Q T C Q K Y I O T
M Q O D V U O S I L E S T S
Q O H T O S E L E N E T L H
Q T T M B U A W N L S E G I
W A P S T S Z K C J I M M L
I K A L E K A L H E L S Y A
R A C V Y L N B J U P Q I B
R F V X G N A L E H P L G F
L E T L A K A L A L O S O M
O S I Š T N A O Š T I L M T
R A K H A B A N E Z G O E H
S E K O N Y A N A A A Q U B I
```

KHABANE	HOSE
LESOTHO	LETLAKALA
MOTSELA	MOSOLA
SETS'ELISI	SEFAKA
DITSHILA	SEKONYANA
PHELANG	PEO
TS'ELISO	MBUA
LIPALESA	LITŠOANTŠISO
LEHLAKELA	METSI

43 - Herbalism

```
Z Q J K B G I X A L E S A B
O X A O K A R O M D K P I H
X L P N K D O Z P T I A S M
N E E O B H U Z V W N R R O
F C Š F O N A G E R O S O L
E C T O A A S H C K R L S E
Y S O L P N E F L D F E E M
R E D E V A L Y E I A X M O
M I N T K H A P N G S F A N
B H I X N A P X N I R O R A
D Q C E A N I P E G A N Y M
Y K D V P O L C F Z D R V A
T R F W U M S E M E L A T T
M O E K E T S I L Q T L W U
```

MORAKOA
BASELA
MOLEMO
KHAHLISO
FENNEL
TAMANO
LIPALESA
TŠEPA
KONOFOLE

MONAHANA
MOEKETSI
LAVEDER
MINT
OREGANO
PARSLE
SEMELA
ROSEMARY
SAFRONIKE

44 - Vehicles

```
R S Y F D J O T U H T V D S
A X N X N I S E K E T Z S E
S M E N V D I B J N S S V K
M E B Y K G L I N A R E T E
O T F U F O E R N O L Y B P
E E I O L U S I D S G Q E E
K K T F F E T J U T O D K P
E O K M C A S B A E K E L A
T R S K N O N E T E R E K A
S A T O K O K E S F K U W V
I I E K O L O I H C K Z R A
E B B H E L I K O P E L E N
L I E K E T S E N G R A F T
M O T S A M A I I S U C Q Q
```

SEFOFANE	RAFT
AMBULESE	ROKETE
BAEKELA	SEKOKOTA
SEKEPE	TS'ELISO
BESE	TEKESI
KOLOI	LIEKETSENG
TS'OANE	TEBIRI
MOEKETSI	THUTO
HELIKOPELE	TEREKA
MOTSAMAI	VAN

45 - Flowers

```
Q Z U X K A G B Z E I T L M
H R P A L E B O S E L U F S
X S J N E Q M X T K J L R E
Z U Q O T P P M F O T I E Z
A C B E S E U L O L I P D F
L S L P A L D O L O J I E L
S I W Y T I A L N B W S V Q
J B L O S L A I N E D R A G
A I G Y I A M P R T K U L C
S H K E C K S O E E A I P K
M O R C H I D P Z W M Q E F
I D A N D E L I O N E U T B
N M A G N O L I A Y X B L P
E N A B A H K L H Y Q J A P
```

KHABANE	LILY
KOLOBE	MAGNOLIA
LETSATSI	ORCHID
DANDELIONE	PEONA
GARDENIA	PETLA
HIBISCUS	PLUMERIA
JASMINE	POPI
LAVEDER	LESOBELA
LILAK	TULIPI

46 - Health and Wellness #1

```
J  P  J  O  S  T  A  H  T  O  H  K  M  S
O  L  A  L  T  E  L  K  J  A  N  O  O  S
M  F  X  I  S  A  M  A  K  A  H  P  R  E
E  A  J  I  K  I  N  I  L  K  O  Z  I  B
A  O  S  T  A  M  U  R  H  A  K  I  A  E
M  P  O  A  N  Y  Q  E  O  G  W  F  N  L
Y  B  H  L  P  K  Z  T  D  N  K  C  A  I
G  B  N  E  D  O  L  K  C  S  U  F  W  S
N  O  L  I  K  E  O  A  F  E  P  X  D  A
X  L  T  R  D  O  Z  B  M  O  K  H  O  A
O  E  L  I  H  O  M  O  N  E  N  O  G  U
U  M  D  S  S  B  T  S  E  L  I  S  O  F
G  O  T  A  V  A  E  R  A  S  E  H  G  U
I  Y  B  M  P  H  O  M  P  H  O  K  X  V
```

SEBELISA	TS'ELISO
BAKTERIA	MORIANA
MASAPO	MASIRI
KLINIKI	MATS'OA
NGAKA	PHAKAMASI
KHOTHATSO	MAEMO
MOKHOA	PHOMPHO
BOLEMO	LETLALO
LIHOMONE	PHEKO
TLALA	VAERASE

47 - Town

```
M U I D A T S N U S T T O V
P U M A R E K A V U Š M C D
P H S S F O H V V P E A X Y
S A A E W K A K N A B C K O
E K L K M V R H G M E G H S
F H S E A O O Z D A L H D I
O A E T S M G N E K E B E L
F L K I I A A E L E T O H H
A E O S Q X C S I T S S M A
I L L E N Y Y I I E O Q Y H
Y E O V B A K E R E K E V K
R J P I S T E K E O M X C Q
I K I N I L K Y Y O W Q G G
N N C U N S K A U L Y B J N
```

SEFOFA
BAKEREKE
BANKA
KHAHLISO
KLINIKI
PALESA
KHALELE
HOTELE
MOEKETSI
MAREKA

MUSEMO
PHAKAMASI
SEKOLO
STADIUM
LEBEKENG
SUPAMAKETE
TŠEBELETSO
UNIVESITE
ZOO

48 - Antarctica

```
L L E Q E K O A Y V H D Z O
T E M O T S E A N E O A F R
I B T L I H L A K E N G A K
K Y G S G E O G R A F I Q M
O V C B O Y L E R U U T D I
L K J E S A C Z R W I O Q F
O I H D T P E N I N S U L A
H M D A E N A B A H K V K R
O E Y C L O P Z U K T R E G
P T S S E A I A M A S T Z O
O S V A K N S F B Q J A W P
H I A P E S T I L E E N B O
K L M U L A O P F Z L K A T
L I N O N Y A N A W P O Y N
```

BAY
LINONYANA
LERUU
PABELO
KHABANE
KHOPO
TIKOLOHO
LEKELETSO
GEOGRAFI
KHALASI

LEQEKOA
LIHLAKENGA
TSAMAI
LITS'EPA
PENINSULA
LETS'OA
MOTS'EANE
TOPOGRAFI
METSI

49 - Ballet

```
B A T H E E L E T S I N A Q
M T S E L I S O T E T L W N
L A M O K H O A O O N I M M
Y N S J O Q T P T S O T Z R
P L F I A O O X Q T S E Z B
E I J I R J W K O E T B T A
L M Q A J I N N E O A O S T
S H U C U M X J Q S H H E L
I P A L H O M Q W T T O B I
D U H P Y J D Y K S O R O S
T Š O E L E T S O I H R A I
J A M S T G F O M T K G B S
M O E K E T S I W S Z O V I
O I O C O H T O M O H T O M
```

LITEBOHO
BATHEELETSI
MOHLAPI
BATLISISI
TŠOELETSO
TS'ITSO
MOHAU
KHOTHATSO
MASIRI

MMINO
OKESTRA
TS'ELISO
TS'OETSOE
MOTHO MOTHO
TSEBO
MOKHOA
MOEKETSI

50 - Fashion

```
M V G O U T W T E S L W K I
L O S I L E Š T A M N I Q P
I S K M O K H O A P E S E L
K I M H L I A P A R O C Y X
O L X V A O E S T O M E A N
N E V N G B M O N Y A N E L
A S V P J Y I T E B E L L O
N T L D G N E S T E K E I L
E N A B A H K A O P B B K P
T S E L I S I T S O E O V F
B O I H L O K O F B Q N U X
Q F E F G E U Q I T U O B G
T L H O K O M E L O N L H N
B D L F Y E N A O S T O M Q
```

TS'ELISITSOE
BOUTIQUE
LIKONANE
LIAPARO
MATŠELISO
KHABANE
MOKHABISO
TEBELLO
LESEPA
LACE

LIEKETSENG
MONYANE
MOTS'OANE
BOIHLOKO
TS'ELISO
MOTS'EOA
BONOLO
MOKHOA
TLHOKOMELO

51 - Human Body

```
H M T P K N M L M F M D L S
O L O K N C A E O K O B E E
M Y O L E P L H L X H J T T
O J K O A I I A O M L C L S
N Q N P H L L T M Q A C A O
O B V A H O A L O W H F L E
A M H S A J E A F P A G O B
N L R A O D V V U S R I I E
A K G M L E L O G N E L U S
U H S E F A H L E H O B X T
C H I N N A D K R L E T A O
V J W N V L Z L E G S K L P
L E T S O H O X V U X K E P
Z U T A I K Z Y C A C B S R
```

NKOLO
MALI
MASAPO
BOKO
CHINNA
TSEBE
SETS'OE
SEFAHLEHO
MONOANA
LETSOHO

HLOOHO
PELO
MOHLAHARE
LENGOLE
LETAO
MOLOMO
MOLALA
NKO
LEHATLA
LETLALO

52 - Musical Instruments

```
J B Z A T E P M O R E T K D
K Z A E S O N K O M T I R R
E L C S S B E H J T N Z B B
X V N N O O P C N E H I R A
N M F I K O O S A N N E P N
B H I W V H A X B I W M R A
K A T A R A A F Y R A A A O
V I O L I N I N Y A M R H K
M A N D O L I N G L Y I U A
S A X O P H O N E C R M D L
L E H L O H O N O L O B T H
P I A N O Q G V Y U Z A Y E
T Š E B E L E T S O Q Q J L
R J Z C E L L O I H C V D T
```

BANJO	MANDOLIN
BASOOA	MARIMBA
CELLO	OBOE
CLARINET	LEHLOHONOLO
MOTHERO	PIANO
LEHLAKOANA	SAXOPHONE
KHANG	TŠEBELETSO
KATARA	TEROMPETA
HARP	VIOLIN

53 - Fruit

```
P K S I R I L A M U N U G V
A H N E C T A R I N E R U F
P Ó S N E K D P U D E M A E
A K M A B O L I L A N E V I
Y H P E R E K I S I H V A E
A Ó Q I T E C W G Y P A V Q
K N H G U L D I P E R E G X
O A U I P O E K O D S R S L
C T L B F P L E H A P U E O
H E L O P A N A N A B Q F B
E F M G J N R L T L S S E K
R K M N C I W O D A C O V A
I Z C A Y E D M M Q V G P R
X J B M S P R A S P B E R I
```

APOLE	KIWI
MABOLILANE	SIRILAMUNU
AVOCADO	MANGO
BANANA	LEHAPU
BERRY	NECTARINE
CHERI	PAPAYA
KHÓKHÓNATE	PEREKISI
FEIE	PERE
MORAFI	PEINAPOLE
GUAVA	RASPBERI

54 - Engineering

```
L  R  E  T  E  M  A  I  D  Y  G  U  L  M
I  P  O  S  I  A  M  A  S  T  B  D  E  O
E  A  B  O  S  T  A  H  T  O  H  K  K  Q
K  K  E  A  K  P  A  W  H  S  P  O  O  E
E  O  T  N  A  E  H  P  H  I  X  K  L  T
T  L  O  E  F  N  H  G  B  L  C  U  A  S
S  A  B  R  I  A  K  P  S  E  L  H  G  I
E  C  G  E  V  H  P  E  D  S  F  N  L  P
N  G  T  K  D  E  Y  A  L  T  A  M  Z  C
G  K  P  E  O  S  T  E  L  E  B  E  Š  T
N  N  T  I  O  T  I  A  M  A  S  T  O  M
G  Z  E  L  H  O  R  T  K  E  Q  E  O  I
H  J  N  O  A  M  K  A  B  E  L  O  U  I
F  D  S  Y  K  S  E  B  O  P  E  H  O  S
```

PHEKO	TS'OANE
KELESE	LIEKERE
PAKOLA	LIEKETSENG
KAHOO	MOQETSI
BOTEBO	MOTS'EHANE
TŠEBELETSO	LEKOLA
DIAMETER	MOTSAMAI
TS'ELISO	KHOTHATSO
KABELO	TSAMAISO
MATLA	SEBOPEHO

55 - Kitchen

```
N X D C O X L G L L L H R R
G A P N S X I S B E I V D Y
W F P E L T T E K B N W M M
L F S K J W H P G A K L O L
I I F B I B I O U K O I T O
D Y K J Z N P N J A M K S S
V I T O S M A E K I F H E T
J U W Z B G K N H U L O L E
A P R O N E B G A L W P I L
S E I T S A N E H R F O S E
F E R E K O S V L M V M I B
S E K O P I Y D I O V A N E
K H A B A N E A L Q I A P Š
W I V E D Y G C E F B T Z T
```

APRON	LITHIPA
SEKOPI	LEBAKA
LIKHOPO	NAPKIN
LIKOBE	OVANE
LIJO	TŠEBELETSO
FEREKO	SEITSANE
MOTS'ELISI	LINKO
KHAHLILE	SEPONENG
JUG	KHABANE
KETTLE	

56 - Government

```
N T L E T Š O A O M W T V T
I V O S T O H K N O X C M E
K M H K A B A H C E S O G M
I D T M O N A K E T E A U O
T N O Q F L F C Y A K O T K
O Š S J O D O G A P E L M E
L Z E O S W S H L E R E O R
O D S B N K X B O L E T L A
P I R I E G R X D E T A A S
I L I L O L H A O M E H O E
L M O A H I E H T P S T T U
M T O L E K O T I D U I H D
M O L A O A J K S B W O E Z
B M O N U M E N T O V B O N
```

MOAHI
SESOTHO
MOLAOTHEO
TEMOKERASE
TŠEBELETSO
SETEREKE
TEKANO
BOITHATELO
MOAHLOLI
TOKA

MOLAOA
MOETAPELE
TOKOLOHO
MONUMENT
SECHABA
KHOTSO
LIPOLOTIKI
DITOKELO
PUO
LETŠOAO

57 - Art Supplies

```
Q V I A P G X G R R Y X D N
P M A K A L A O T A G H E A
A X X G T V C V S A S O L I
M A C R Y L I C E L F E I U
P B J S L A R E K A Y O R M
I J C C A B W Y H H X M L P
R G L T H G A P O S T E L E
I T S E L I S O P E E O P L
K A K A M E R A O L N I O E
E M E T S I H M T F K L I S
Q A U C A R F F S A A L G A
Y G S U F U W P O O C N Q P
L D A E C L I T Š O A N E I
W E S E L M M A K H O P O I
```

ACRYLIC	SEKHOPOTSO
LITŠOANE	MAKHOPO
KAKAMERA	ENKA
TS'ELISO	OLI
LESHALA	PAMPIRI
LETSOPA	PASELE
MAKALA	TAFOLE
EASEL	METSI
RASER	

58 - Science Fiction

```
X  S  O  T  O  B  O  R  I  L  C  M  H  C
Q  I  Y  I  C  X  M  R  T  S  J  O  P  W
T  O  N  C  P  J  O  U  A  E  Z  L  B  W
N  S  A  R  W  W  T  Z  M  C  G  L  N  T
F  I  E  S  A  K  A  M  I  L  L  O  W  H
G  L  T  L  K  H  A  L  A  X  E  E  U  E
L  H  E  T  I  T  S  I  R  U  T  U  F  K
I  A  N  K  S  S  K  H  A  B  A  N  E  N
B  H  A  W  T  I  I  M  O  L  H  O  M  O
U  K  L  A  A  W  E  T  E  E  Y  T  Y  L
K  H  P  L  O  S  X  T  S  U  Y  T  N  O
A  I  P  O  T  U  J  B  S  O  P  J  D  J
D  Y  S  T  O  P  I  A  G  O  E  Y  X  I
Y  C  T  T  S  O  A  L  A  N  G  Q  A  Q
```

ATOMO
LIBUKA
LIMAKASE
KHAHLISO
DYSTOPIA
KHABANE
TS'ELISITSOE
MOLLO
FUTURISTI

KHALAXE
TSIETSO
TS'OALANG
MOHLOMI
ORACLE
PLANETE
LIROBOTO
THEKNOLOJI
UTOPIA

59 - Geometry

```
K I E K V F K K U C H L X T
M A S I S A A H I A F J B A
Z N Q A H L R A K A B E S K
R E B M U N O B P H E K O T
C B X A D T L A M B Q E M Z
C O O S L I O N P A K O L A
J L A T W E A E E X P S K L
S E W O U L K M V F G T A T
X M E M V M I A E J A N N E
J O S T O P O H K T Z A A Y
R A D I U S E Q E A E M N N
T Š E B E L E T S O R R E O
T S E L I S I T S O E E L M
A Y P H A P A N G G F K O H
```

PHEKO
PAKOLA
DIAMETER
TŠEBELETSO
KHABANE
BOLEMO
MANTSOE
MASISA
MOTSAMAI
NUMBER

PHAPANG
TS'ELISITSOE
MONYETLA
KAROLO
RADIUSE
LEKAKARE
SEBAKA
KANANELO
KHOPOTSO

60 - Airplanes

```
W D M S T S E L I S O B T F
I P O K E S C S M B O O S B
F T T F O B U C U S G I O O
H F S O S T A R O M M T A L
R T A L H A L K V T O U N E
Q S M I V Q H H A S S M E M
W O A M A F U R A A E E L O
K A I S T E K E O M B L O P
E N A O L O L A B A E O M H
G E X J C E E M V I T O Y E
M O T S E L I S I S S H D K
X C X I G J H L L A I A M O
P H A T L A L A T S A K K A
L A X W H D W C X P G N Y S
```

BOITUMELO	MAFURA
MOEA	BOLEMO
PHEKOA	TS'OANELO
SEBAKA	PHATLALATSA
BALOLOANE	LAHLA
KAHOO	TSAMAISA
MOSEBETSI	MOEKETSI
TS'ELISO	MOTSAMAI
MORATSO	SEKOPI
TS'OANE	MOTS'ELISI

61 - Ocean

```
A S G O H A W M J M K O M N
K L H D E I K A U A O C O T
O T G R Y W L T L T R T H L
G L N A I E N S C Š A O L I
K H E O E M S O M O L P A H
Y A N T P D P S C E E H K L
J P O R E O H O Q L W A O A
S I P E K Q N Z U E M S L P
E N E E E L J I S R J E A I
F O S F S W E L H C X U R T
E H O Y S T E R A P T U N A
F A T E A L A H K E L Y E C
O N Y N R O X O A Q B O C V
I A W S T E L F N F X A D M
```

ALGAE
SEKEPE
KORALE
LEKHALA
DOLPHIN
TLHAPINOHANA
LIHLAPI
OCTOPHASE
OYSTER
REEF

LETSWAI
SHAKA
SHRIMP
SEPONENG
SEFEFO
MATŠOELE
TUNA
KGOKA
MATSOSO
MOHLAKOLA

62 - Force and Gravity

```
M G G U T H O L O A N A F K
H A L H I F K H A T E L L O
L A K A B E S R Y O M T Q U
A N L A K E K E T S O F U N
L K I M N L I P A N E T I O
E T H C D E K E L E S E K S
L D S O O S T E L E B E Š T
E T S E H Y J E J C T R Z E
T P Y X L A N A K O S V B R
S S R O G A N H H B I V Q A
O O L T O L T E L S T C A K
L I E K E T S E N G S N J A
D I S T A N C E C B O A C P
M O H L O M I L E B E L O S
```

KELESE	TS'ITSO
SEBAKA	TSELA
HLALELETSO	FIHLA
DISTANCE	LIPANETI
MOHLOMI	KHATELLO
KEKETSO	LETLOTLO
KHOHANE	LEBELO
TŠEBELETSO	NAKO
MAKANETE	PAKARETSO
LIEKETSENG	THOLOANA

63 - Birds

```
E B N L K A N A N E L O P A
I M D E P E L I C A N H B Z
P W C K P E N G U I N E S F
N A E H E L Z F U F T R N V
S A E O G N I M A L F O K Z
L T B B N A R Y N M P N O O
E A O E K C I Z A O K I D O
K T R R Q U H U W K H F K G
H E E E K O P H S H O R I O
A L S Q O T M W T O H B T T
N W M Y N X L M E O O K O K
T W V W P T B R S K Q L V S
S H C Q H A S V X O J W O I
Í P A K A M A U K A N K B B
```

KANANELO	HERON
KHOHO	MPHIRI
MOKHOOKOA	PAKAMA
KOKOO	PIKO
LETATA	PELICAN
NTSU	PENGUIN
LEHE	SEROBE
FLAMINGO	STORK
LEKHANTSÍ	SETSWANA
LEKHOBE	TOUCAN

64 - Nutrition

```
C E S A P J T P H E L A N G
H L Z N U O I S H M U R X P
E V B T Y Y F R E R D T X O
F B P H O L O S O L W G A N
O O B S M T K P N L I O D A
K A O S O S T H A K A S I N
B O H L O K O E M H J K O A
P H E K O B T P A A X E I O
H K R G S R G H T B B W S L
W E T L O P N I M A T I V O
Y M A A S V I L Y N Y B W H
E V G A O S T E L E K E L T
M A K A B O H Y D R A T E X
L I E K E T S E N G A H S I
```

LEKELETSO	PHOLOSO
BOHLOKO	PHEPHILE
LIKALORI	LIEKETSENG
MAKABOHYDRATE	PHEKO
JESO	KHABANE
TS'ELISO	SOSO
PHELANG	CHEFO
TSOSOA	VITAMIN
TAMANO	THOLOANA
MEKHOA	

65 - Hiking

```
D S G X I V N A X R B F G Q
I Y P A M H L A H A F F M F
S E H L O H O T S E L I S O
T E S E H S M P C O W L M T
A B G M A Z T O V V H C A H
S R N O H G L A T I B H T A
T Q O L L D P L H S L M S B
E B O H T Q D I Z T A T O E
L I P A K A K A C O A M A N
L E S O T H O V T K X H A G
F O L O F O O H P I L Y K I
L I B U T S O V K L L K K D
P W L I T S E L I S I N V Y
P H A K I S O M E T S I E F
```

LIPHOOFOLO	TLHAHO
LIBUTSO	TS'ELISO
MOTSAMAI	LIPAKAKA
CLIFF	PHAKISO
LESOTHO	MATS'OA
LITS'ELISI	SEHLOHO
LIKOTSI	LETSATSI
HLOMELA	KHATHATSO
MAP	METSI
THABENG	HLAHA

66 - Professions #1

```
M V R T M S Q F A D E M R M
M O L Z G O E N A I P O A O
O B T S P G T T A D T P M E
H A L S J W V L S O O E O K
L N K K E I L S A O N L L E
A K M V N L E C W T M I A T
N A O N A E I C P C S I O S
K K H O E B A S T B U I S I
A A L I S I M I I K E L G O
N G A Q T H A K A G N O U K
Y X K T O T S P U L A L E K
A Z A K M A T X R I B H H B
N B N I K O O M I W U O Z V
E U E V D M M E E U Y M Q U
```

MOTS'ELISI	MOHLAKANE
MOHLANKANYANE	RAMOLAO
MOATHIBELI	MOPELI
MOEKETSI	MOOKI
BANKAKA	PIANE
MOTSAMAI	PULA
NGAKA	MOTS'EANE
MOHLOLI	MOTLATSI
SETSOMI	

67 - Barbecues

```
M E R O T S O J K F C A L T
M H I J K N D Y H G N O I S
X X O R M A N A O L O H T H
J S O N S E P N H Z T M H E
M M I N O B E T O E T B I B
L U L E L L A O S T O M P E
L I S R A M T N Z X K A A T
M Z J J B W A P A L E L S S
X Y R O W Y T W H S R K A A
B T L E T S W A I O E H L Z
L E H L A B U L A S F O A O
L I P A P A L I Q O V T T E
R T Š E B E L E T S O S E Q
T L A L A H A A K H H O D D
```

KHOHO
BANA
TŠEBELETSO
LELAPA
LIJO
FEREKO
MOTSOALLE
THOLOANA
LIPAPALI
KHOTSO

TSHEBETSA
TLALA
LITHIPA
MMINO
SALATE
LETSWAI
SOSO
LEHLABULA
TATAE
MEROTSO

68 - Chocolate

```
O P R B T K L A T S O A N G
C R R O S H I S T E K E O M
N Q B H E A P E T A N O M Y
Y E I L B B M H A R M W N N
T O I O E A R Q O G I A I H
T S K K L N A Y T O F H N G
H T E O E N N A S F C L O
A E V L X O N O R F Y O V J
B L P B I E N A O E P I L Y
E E L D P S L E M A R A K O
L B K Q I R O L A K I L S G
E E A N T I O X I D A N T F
N Š I E S M S C A C A O Y B
G T K H Ó K H Ó N A T E F I
```

ANTIOXIDANT
BOHLOKO
CACAO
LIKALORI
KARAMEL
KHÓKHÓNATE
THABELENG
TS'ELISO
MORATOA

TAMANO
MOEKETSI
LIPEOANE
PHOOFOLO
KHABANE
TŠEBELETSO
TS'EBELE
MONATE
LATSOANG

69 - Vegetables

```
K L T H I B A K A B S K B R
K O N E X E B R A H E L M Z
H E N K Z R T N A L P G G E
R U P O K O M Y N I I R G T
K Q T H F M B C A T N A H A
I L O C C O R B M M I D K L
R A L I R K L T A U C I S A
E N L T D O L E H S H S E S
L Y A R L M H L T H I E H W
E A H A S O U S A R I N O J
S N S X E K S R M O V H E A
B E L O U P Z A A O S Q T L
J S J Q H D Q P T M B X E P
W E A O A L O F I L O H K B
```

ARTICHOKE	ANYANESE
BROCCOLI	PARSLE
SEHOETE	PEA
KHOLIFOLAOA	MOKOPU
SELERI	RADISE
KOMOKOMORE	SALATE
EGGPLANT	SHALLOT
KONOFOLE	SEPINICHI
THAMANA	TAMATI
MUSHROOM	THIBAKA

70 - Boats

```
I S I L E S T O M Y C B S H
S A E M A T S E L A V U A O
T H E K K A Y A K D V O I Y
E A U A E O N A K J L Y S O
K T R S T P S Z T O G V T K
E L T T P A E Š T E Š T E L
O P E A J L U S O E C H B R
M A T O K O K P E D V C E I
R I F H A M B P L K K A S Q
C N A K A T X M R B E Y O F
W X R E G P L Q D Z J P M M
C E A L C B O A O R O H E I
L E K H O T L A T S O A N E
L E O E T L E N A T H O L I
```

LEKHOTLA	NATHOLI
BUOY	LEOETLE
KANOE	RAFT
MOSEBETSI	MOLAPO
KOKO	THAPO
TS'OANE	SEKEPE SEKEPE
MOEKETSI	MOTS'ELISI
KAYAK	LEOATLA
LETŠETŠE	LEKHOATSA
MATSELA	YACHT

71 - Driving

```
X  J  D  F  P  A  M  L  T  S  E  L  A  L
T  Z  K  M  O  K  O  L  O  I  N  M  A  E
L  L  Z  B  L  T  B  F  E  H  A  O  L  S
Q  E  B  F  O  W  E  U  C  U  N  T  E  E
N  B  T  X  K  M  M  R  T  X  O  S  P  K
I  G  D  S  O  Q  I  L  E  J  H  A  O  A
I  C  P  M  E  B  A  N  E  K  K  M  L  N
K  H  A  S  E  L  M  E  M  B  A  A  E  E
K  O  T  S  I  J  A  J  A  A  E  I  S  N
V  E  X  J  B  E  S  E  F  F  V  L  A  G
K  A  R  A  R  E  T  I  U  O  V  B  O  B
M  A  T  Š  O  E  L  E  R  L  E  E  L  X
L  J  N  S  N  T  K  W  A  Z  Z  A  B  N
S  E  T  H  U  U  T  H  U  A  H  J  J  B
```

MATŠOELE	SETHUUTHU
BESE	LEPOLESA
KOLOI	TSELA
KOTSI	POLOKO
MAFURA	LEBELO
KARARE	LETSELA
KHASE	TSAMAI
LESEKANENG	TEREKA
MAP	KHONANE
MOTSAMAI	

72 - Professions #2

```
M L E W N V R I M M M L P M
L O E S P K L T O O O K O O
L H L N G D N A S P H W W E
Y S T E I O M O U E L D Z K
I Z X V M N H E O P A G M E
L I P U O I O O E I L M O T
M O T S E L I S I T E O T S
Z H O X V E D T L O F H S I
C B N Y W L Z O F L I L A Z
K J B S T E A M R I U A M I
X R K F A K A G N L O B A T
C R Q X B O Q G C O O I I N
G N E L I M E H K M R S P C
T Š E B E L E T S O G A S K
```

MOTSAMAI	LIPUO
KHEMILENG	MOPEPI
LENINO	MOHLALEFI
MOEKETSI	NGAKA
MOLEMI	MOLILOTI
MOHLABI	TŠEBELETSO
MOKELELI	MOSUOE
MOTS'ELISI	MOTS'OEOATI

73 - Mythology

```
C B H M F V I X T A L B M Z
G F S O L U O P M R E O O J
J N Q H X U M S O C B I H S
T B E A T R I F N H E T L C
L S V L I U B F A E T Š O X
E S O E E J A W T T S O M T
H E S A L F M K E Y A A I U
O A T T N F A I A P N R S M
L D E E X E B S H E A O T E
I U L C U H L T O P O P A L
M M E M Z I X O L B K O L O
O A S E Q B N K V C M P T C
N K U I C D S E T S O K O E
G I P S E H L O B O H O M W
```

ARCHETYPE
BOITŠOARO
TUMELO
POPO
SEHLOBOHO
SETSO
MABIMO
KOTSI
LEHOLIMONG
MOHALE

BOSAFELENG
POULO
LEBETSANA
TS'OANELO
MOTLATSI
MONATE
MOHLOMI
PUSELETSO
SEADUMA

74 - Hair Types

```
M K H A N Y A Q X H L K P X
R A S T E M O Y B G I H H K
A R L X T Š O E U C K U E Q
T E C A O O S T O B H T P L
S F R W T O S U S X A S H E
O E J Z U S D B J V L A I F
E L Q V J T I T F W A N L A
W I O O U U A Š B E D E E T
T S Y W L P R O L O N O B L
Y S N I W O B A G H D O H A
S C O G Z M F N T E L E L E
R N R A O O S E L V V W Z X
F W C Q N H A R E L A N E H
S N A O L E M O K O H L T W
```

LEFATLA	MOPUTSO
TŠOANE	PHEPHILE
LESOOA	TELELE
RATSOE	KHANYA
BRAIDS	KHUTSANE
BOTSOOA	SILEFERA
MALATSI	BONOLO
LIKHALA	TS'OANE
HARELANE	TLHOKOMELO
OMETSA	TŠOEU

75 - Furniture

```
L V F K P O L F J D Y A A K
X E N Z I S I L E Š T O M A
V U B N Q O K O M M A H O O
R U G O K L E L E O Š T A M
H Z L T N G K P L D S W D A
I P H U P A E H I U E W E S
V N X F D E T E E D H H S O
A L M F F E S K K O L T E M
S E B O N E O O E B A S K N
M O T S A M A I T E B E O W
T S O A N E L O S N A L A D
M O T L A T S I E S K I D G
L I S H E P H E N E A S Y F
O G B F F S Y B G Y Q O U E
```

SEHLABAKA
PHEKO
BENSE
TS'OANELO
TS'ELISO
MOTŠELISI
MOTSAMAI
LIKEKETSO
LIEKETSENG
DESEKO

MOTLATSI
FUTON
HAMMOKO
LEBONA
MATŠOELE
SEBONE
MOSAMO
RUG
LISHEPHE

76 - Garden

```
H A M K Y K E X T G O Q J M
T O L E V A D W Š F N T Z A
Š S S C E R A C E S N E B P
E T J E A A S H P G S O U H
B E E J E R T W A N M X F E
E L N P U E A O L B S Q A K
L D I I N T R K H V N F S O
E A L G Z A A O A K A F E S
T L O T O F H M L B E Z L N
S A P M T E K M H O O L A T
O L M O B S U A E J Q R P K
D H A R A K E H S A Y H I U
M O R A F I Z E E N S W L M
J M T M O F O K A G J E K R
```

BENSE	SEFAKA
SEHLAHLA	LETS'OA
LEKHOTA	MAPHEKO
LIPALESA	RAKE
KARARE	KHARATSA
TŠEPA	TŠEBELETSO
BOJANG	TRAMPOLINE
HAMMOKO	SEFATE
HOSE	MORAFI
MOHLALA	MOFOKA

77 - Diplomacy

```
B C T L I P O L O T I K I N
S O I S M O E L E T S I M M
C U T V I Y E D J B L Q O O
V P Y S I E C B R A R L T C
U I H K E C T Q C A D N H H
C L E F H P A S D H Z K O A
H E B V C O E A O I S M M B
P U S O O N A H T O H K O A
T S E B E T S O I Z Q D T T
T Š E B E L E T S O E E H H
T Š E B E L E T S O E O O Y
G T O K A S A O L T N P X S
T H A B E L O S E C H A B A
F T G M O T S E L I S I C M
```

MOELETSI	MOCHABA
MOTS'ELISI	PUSO
BAAHI	MOTHO MOTHO
CIVIC	BOTS'EPEHI
SECHABA	TOKA
KHOTHANO	LIPUO
TS'EBETSO	LIPOLOTIKI
TŠEBELETSOE	TSIETSO
TŠEBELETSO	THABELO
NTLOASA	

78 - Countries #1

```
K A N A N E L A P H Q B V Q
V E N E Z U E L A Q R S O H
B Q Y V I E T N A M R M F G
B R A Z I L E N A M E R E J
S D W I F G I R T B C P S M
L E R H V T Y V E E K T P O
L D O C Y T Q R P T M I A R
S I N E L E A R E S I R I O
E P B Y R G I L G Z O A N C
N O K Y H T N V E P U Q M C
E L G I A E A I T A L I A O
G A C H N N M P A N A M A C
A N X Z K F O F I N L A N D
L D A U G A R A C I N M N T
```

BRAZILE   MOROCCO
KANANELA   NICARAGUA
EGEPETA   NORWAY
FINLAND   PANAMA
JEREMANE   POLAND
IRAQ   ROMANIA
ISERAELE   SENEGAL
ITALIA   SPAIN
LATVIA   VENEZUELA
LIBYA   VIETNAM

79 - Adjectives #1

```
T T W N Q C L T F D M T Z K
L S M O R A K O A P O H L H
H E L K F B H L Y K E A D O
O L F E J N L O K Q K B H T
K I C G B D X H Z T E A L H
O S U H T E N O Q S T N O A
M O F G A O N M E O S G M T
E N A B A H K Y N A I N E S
L L E F I F I J A N Q A L O
O L E N A O S T O E Y H A G
G D G V X G M F S I Z O T J
N Y G N A P E Š T L Y H N S
M D A O K O L H O B J K T W
S N W Y X A E Y M V C G S J
```

KHOTHATSO
KHABANE
MORAKOA
MOEKETSI
KHOHANG
LEFIFI
TS'ELISO
THABANG
HLOMELA

THUSO
TŠEPANG
MOHOLO
TS'OANELO
MOTS'OANE
TLHOKOMELO
LEBENYA
TS'OANE
BOHLOKOA

80 - Rainforest

```
T S A L U U G P X P X L C P
L S B Q U E N A O H K I L U
I B A Y Q K T B H S T M M S
N W H B X T L A P M L B L E
Y A C M A V W L M O H B F L
A E E D R B N L O T A D A E
M D S I B T E O L S H R W T
A M A R U N K L H O O C K S
F A P A N E N G O A P F R O
E O T V A N A Y N O N I L F
I L S L O E N A B A L H E S
G O H T O S E L B H G Z F G
B H L I T Š O A N T Š I S O
P P T L K K Z M S Q X P N N
```

LINONYANA
LESOTHO
MARU
SECHABA
FAPANENG
MOTS'OAOA
LIKHOANE
SEHLABANE
LINYAMA

MOSO
TLHAHO
PABALLO
TS'ABABELO
HLOMPHO
PUSELETSO
LITŠOANTŠISO
PHOLOA

81 - Landscapes

```
L E O S E H L A K A N E T T
C E P I I C E B E R G M U H
U D O V O L C A N O N O N H
H M H E D V E S J V E L D T
X H K R T A Š I N R T A R L
G F O X G L T L B T O P A C
Y K M F A T E H V Q B O X K
D Y V S X A Š A L E E F E L
T H O L A O T H G U L V S M
M P S W E E K G E Y S E R O
O T A D U L L F W W K I N K
P E N I N S U L A J B S N Y
L E H A H A D G N E B A H T
S E K H O P O L O F O O H P
```

LEBOTENG
LEHAHA
LEFEELA
GEYSER
KHAHLISA
THOLA
ICEBERG
SEHLAKANE
LETŠETŠE
THABENG

OASIS
LEOETLE
PENINSULA
MOLAPO
LEOATLA
SEKHOPO
TUNDRA
MOKHOPO
VOLCANO
PHOOFOLO

82 - Visual Arts

```
T L H O K O M E L I S O K L
S E T Š O A N T Š O I L H I
P Q L I K K F I H L A E A E
L E S A E A A S U D U T H K
H E N C P K O T O F E S L E
M L S S C G D E I E N O E R
S A K H E U A K Z P M P J E
T H Y N A L D E F K W A P M
U A C A W L E O J O O A X E
K M F V D I A M A S T O M R
S E T S O A O A U P H F W E
H E P P O N O P O T S O H B
J S L E L E S N E T S I L R
O D P U N V I I E J L D R C
```

MOEKETSI
LIEKEREMERE
KHAHLE
LESHALA
LETSOPA
MOTSAMAI
TLHOKOMELISO
EASEL
FIHLA
SEEMAHALE

PEKO
PEN
PENSELE
PONO POTSO
SEFOTO
SETŠOANTŠO
SETS'OAOA
STENSELE
KAKA

83 - Plants

```
Z U Q D G B M A P Q R Z C L
X S I B A P E Š T E C R H E
L S R Y M F T R O S T O M H
L I P A L E S A R Z M L C L
F L F K X W R J P Y E J A A
S G N A J O B Q Q Z H J E K
I K R B C A C T U S L R N E
X F F I S T A S T E A K A L
T O C L I R G A Z N Z S Y A
Z K Z D B H B I M A M H N N
S X C U P J M A O O B M A B
F S E H L A H L A N S W T A
S E F A T E M T S O H O O I
I V Y F L O R A G M D L B I
```

BAMBOO	MEHLA
LIBAKA	TŠEPA
BERRY	BOJANG
BOTANYANE	IVY
SEHLAHLA	MOSO
CACTUS	PETLA
MONOANE	MOTSO
FLORA	STEM
LIPALESA	SEFATE
LEHLAKELA	TSATSI

84 - Boxing

```
L J G N A L A H T A H K I Y
Y I B O A F I L E F E L E M
I X E F B H P K Z F U G T O
S L P K A N J P H R V K S T
T E J B E N L G D O W K E S
A L T D K T X F J K P R B A
L E Z S D Q S W D N R O O M
T B O E O W M E M M E L E A
O E G I E E D A N N I H C I
M S Y A W Q T N S G B H S B
K H A N Y A J O K A L T O P
B Z T Q X P E K M A T L A Z
P M O H A N Y E T S I J W U
T S E L I S O S I B E S T D
```

SEBELE
MMELE
CHINNA
SEK'ONA
SETS'OE
KHATHALANG
MOTSAMAI
LEFELE
TSEBISO

KHANYA
MOHANYETSI
LIEKETSENG
POTLAKO
TS'ELISO
MOTLATSI
LIKHOPO
TSEBO
MATLA

85 - Countries #2

```
E T H I O P I A L M I C W A
Q O J E A F Z L P E T T J L
C X F S D I L I C X M S A B
L P Z V N F R B E I B O M A
K E M E A M V E R C H M A N
V N B N G U D R G O C A I I
O A N A U J E I C I P L C A
Q P A D N X L A P E N I A U
M A T U E E S U R C O A G K
F J S S B N C Q G E G X H R
H A I T I R M N L E M C C A
Y J K L A O S A E R U P D I
A H A S Y R I A R G U T P N
A B P M P W O Z H K C F B E
```

ALBANIA
DENMARK
ETHIOPIA
GREECE
HAITI
JAMAICA
JAPANE
LAOS
LEBANE
LIBERIA

MEXICO
NEPAL
NIGERIA
PAKISTAN
RUSE
SOMALIA
SUDANE
SYRIA
UGANDA
UKRAINE

86 - Ecology

```
M  T  S  A  T  S  I  F  C  W  K  P  X  T
P  A  O  L  O  H  P  T  U  D  H  T  L  S
Y  R  R  K  G  N  E  N  A  P  A  F  I  E
S  O  L  E  O  H  A  H  L  T  B  G  C  L
M  L  W  M  K  M  A  L  E  M  I  L  H  I
L  F  R  H  B  A  E  V  T  X  T  R  A  S
E  F  A  U  N  A  N  L  T  J  A  N  B  I
F  M  A  R  E  K  A  E  O  E  G  Q  A  T
A  L  I  T  Š  O  A  N  T  Š  I  S  O  S
T  M  O  S  E  B  E  T  S  I  Y  I  Y  O
Š  F  T  L  I  T  H  A  B  E  N  G  H  E
E  A  T  B  L  E  S  O  T  H  O  C  P  N
J  D  B  O  I  T  H  A  T  E  L  O  N  U
P  H  I  V  T  J  C  U  R  R  W  L  L  M
```

LESOTHO	LITHABENG
LICHABA	TLHAHO
FAPANENG	LIMELA
KOMELO	MOSEBETSI
FAUNA	LITŠOANTŠISO
FLORA	PHOLOA
LEFATŠE	TS'ELISITSOE
KHABITA	TSATSI
MAREKANE	BOITHATELO
MAREKA	

87 - Adjectives #2

```
R P A S T A L T A M L S T H
O H Y W L L R I T L I U U L
B E N A B A H K V C M Z M A
A P T E Q S H A J I P W E L
L H M Š M T Z S H B H Z L O
A I V H E E G I Q O O L O S
I L A L B B E L U X M E P I
O E K A I E E A V N X T O G
Y M V H Y H X L W N L S H U
V I E A V S M H E G N W K F
F V J T Q T X C M T V A O B
H I Q Z S Q H C R K S I M I
M O C H A A Y N A H K O L O
T T H A B A N G T L A L A A
```

TŠEBELETSO	THABANG
MOKHOPO	TLHAHO
HLALOSI	MOCHA
OMETSA	HLALISA
KHABANE	KHANYA
TUMELO	LETSWAI
LIMPHO	ROBALA
PHEPHILE	MATLATSA
TSHEBETSA	HLAHA
TLALA	

88 - Psychology

```
M A K H O P O V T L X Z J K
C K S E J U F S L P A B I H
V O K P G E J Y I H T D O E
Z L L J E O K N E S A D S T
S E G O L E M O K O H L T H
E L L H Y K R E S T L E I
B O O K R B A O T O O I L S
E P A N A O S T S S B K E O
L P S V A E C I E T P E B Z
E G T A F H Y L N A H L E Z
C M K I N P T O G M E E Š Y
K A N A N E L O I U K T T Y
M O T H O M O T H O O S U E
M O T S E L I S I K W O T F
```

KHETHISO	LIEKETSENG
KANANELO	MAKHOPO
TS'OANA	POLELO KA
MOTS'ELISI	MOTHO MOTHO
TLHOKOMELO	BOTHATA
KHOTHANO	SEBELE
LITORO	TŠEBELETSO
EGO	PHEKO
MATSOSO	LIKELETSO

89 - Math

```
G T M A L O K A L H O M A P
S S A S I L A M I C E D R E
S E K D A G N A P A H P I R
A L H U X I A E K W C P T I
R I O J N R N V M J R O H M
I S A I S T E K E O M L M E
K O N H J E L T I B C Y E T
R A E O F M O Z E A K O T E
B A R M T O T T H M U N I R
O K D O F E A I E J A E K K
L A W I H G Q I J C P I I L
U B E V U A G S P Z I J D V
M E K I Y S N K H A B A N E
O S Q F Q L E O L A P I L P
```

MAKHOANE   LIPALO
ARITHMETIKI   PHAPANG
DECIMALI   PERIMETER
DIAMETER   POLYONE
KAROHANO   RADIUSE
KHABANE   SEBAKA
MOHLAKOLA   KANANELO
MOEKETSI   TS'ELISO
GEOMETRI   BOLUMO

90 - Water

```
A E O E M T L P U L E N G K
H V R M O M S E C C M Q G H
L M E Z S Z M E O A A F P O
E O S Y O F G A L E E J X L
T F Y Z L S J S H I T F W A
Š O E N A O S T E L S L Q L
E U G Q I M X A Y V J O E A
L F Z K M W O L E N A N A K
A U B Q J F I H R N L I S B
M O L A P O C K L X B N T N
I B O Y K A Y N E O L H E L
N A L E T Š E T Š E M X Q X
M O N A T E H F B V B I E R
S E T S A N E T P D R Y L M
```

KANANELO	LETŠETŠE
LETŠELA	MOSOLA
MOFOUFU	MOHLOMI
KHOLALA	LEOETLE
SETSANE	PULENG
GEYSER	MOLAPO
MONATE	HLATS'A
LETS'OANE	LEHLOENYA
LEQETSA	STEAM
TS'ELISO	

91 - Activities

```
I  C  S  T  I  Y  U  K  F  L  Q  L  L  T
D  V  E  R  E  M  E  R  E  K  E  I  L  S
V  R  T  A  O  K  O  R  O  M  N  P  J  E
J  I  S  T  E  B  E  S  O  M  K  H  I  B
L  I  P  A  P  A  L  I  T  C  X  O  N  O
Q  U  O  S  I  Š  T  N  A  O  Š  T  I  L
K  H  A  B  A  N  E  C  N  T  W  O  X  J
L  I  E  K  E  T  S  E  N  G  Š  U  L  Q
T  P  H  O  M  P  H  O  K  E  P  O  N  P
S  Š  M  O  T  S  A  M  A  I  S  D  P  F
A  X  E  K  H  O  T  H  A  L  P  E  Y  I
V  Y  Q  P  T  S  E  L  I  S  O  U  D  T
H  R  Q  F  A  O  K  O  L  H  O  B  W  C
L  I  T  H  A  B  E  L  O  N  O  O  V  J
```

MOSEBETSI	KHOTHA
LITŠOANTŠISO	TS'ELISO
MOTSAMAI	BOHLOKOA
LIEKEREMERE	PEKO
LIEKETSENG	LIPHOTO
TŠOPI	KHABANE
LIPAPALI	PHOMPHO
TŠEPA	MOROKOA
TSOMI	TSEBO
LITHABELO	

92 - Business

```
M V L Q C V H T I T A M L P
H I G K T A U V S X C O E T
O S I K E H T E T R A L K M
O I B O N E S T E L N A H O
M F A I A E C E B I O O E K
Z O O M P M O L E M O L T H
K K H D O O N E S Q K I H A
M E T I K T V H O J E M O B
G H O V R F L C M V Š O S A
J T M G Q I D O D P T K T N
T E B E L L O G T N I H E E
K U I P C C A K K L L O T J
L E B E K E N G Z D O S E B
T Š E B E L E T S O K I P E
```

MOKHOSI	PETETSO
TEBELLO	MOLAOLI
KOPANE	MOTHOABI
LITŠEKO	CHELETE
THEKO	OFISI
MOTLOTLO	MOLEMO
MOSEBETSI	THEKISO
MOHIRI	LEBEKENG
MOKHABANE	LEKHETHO
LETSENO	TŠEBELETSO

93 - The Company

```
T  L  I  K  O  T  S  I  R  L  X  T  R  H
S  L  M  O  T  S  A  M  A  I  S  Š  J  X
L  E  H  S  T  A  F  E  L  X  C  E  J  P
L  I  G  O  T  E  Q  P  J  O  G  B  H  R
E  T  E  U  K  J  U  E  R  M  M  E  K  O
K  S  L  K  B  O  P  I  D  A  O  L  H  D
E  O  E  K  E  S  M  M  C  O  K  E  A  U
T  A  P  H  B  T  T  E  L  H  H  T  B  C
S  N  O  O  M  E  S  S  L  K  O  S  A  T
O  E  L  E  U  T  F  E  A  O  P  O  N  M
E  L  E  B  V  E  R  U  N  M  O  Z  E  E
D  O  O  O  D  P  H  P  W  G  X  B  P  V
W  W  S  L  I  T  S  E  L  I  S  O  V  M
B  L  T  M  O  S  E  B  E  T  S  I  E  F
```

KHOEBO	PRODUCT
MOKHOPO	MOTSAMAI
QETO	TSOELO-PELE
MOSEBETSI	KHABANE
LEFATSHE	TŠEBELETSO
TS'OANELO	LEKETSO
PETETSO	LIKOTSI
MOKHOAMO	LITS'ELISO
TLHOKOMELO	LIEKETSENG

94 - Literature

```
Y M P F P A T S E L I S O T
Y Z R O H T O M O H T O M L
J O A L E M O K O L H N L H
T Š E P O T T A M M K A E A
R H Y M E M I S Z R V S B L
S W Y G Z O E S O P R I O O
E N R K N F S W O A Q U K S
H P O R K U I N R I N P O O
L A Y B N T O Z Y E L E I T
O P F R E A J S P V G M L D
O I M F G L M O N G O L I O
H S T I S T E K E O M E V A
O O L T U K I A M O K H O A
K A N A N E L O S T E I S T
```

KANANELO
TS'ELISO
MONGOLI
TŠEPO
PAPISO
HLOKOMELA
TLHALOSO
PUISANO
TS'OANELO
MOFUTA

MOEKETSI
NOBELE
MAIKUTLO
LEBOKO
POETISO
RHYME
MOTHO MOTHO
MOKHOA
SEHLOOHO
TSIETSO

95 - Geography

```
M M N S Q W K X A W Z Y C L
E L O A O M O H K E L Z P E
R E B L H A U D A C A X D B
I B O T A A C J L B M A P O
D O R A O P G N E B A H T E
I K O K K A O Q O K T N Y A
A O A R O B X N A K A B E S
N T R N L P D Y T I C W L T
G O Y Q H U B H L F F R S X
J O L E O Y G M A K A B E L
K U F K B P H A M O S O Y J
S E H L A K A N E B Y S J B
D X D U G F S F C F J F S D
L E O E T L E H S T A F E L
```

LEKHOMO   THABENG
ATLAS   LEBOEA
CITY   LEOETLE
NAHA   LEBAKA
PHAMOSO   MOLAPO
KHABANE   LEOATLA
SEHLAKANE   BOROA
LEBOKO   SEBAKA
MAP   BOHLOKOA
MERIDIAN   LEFATSHE

96 - Pets

```
P L I H L A P I K M N H K T
I U B U E B S D E O G A H F
V W N T F E Y O K K A M O F
W Q O Y Y W X K E H K S L C
N T J A A T A O T O A T A L
L A I F H N N H S L K E L P
L P L M S M A P E U H R A K
I M A R E Y Y S N T O G A A
P E X R L O N L G S O Y B T
O K X K R M A R Q O A S S S
U Y G I K O L N C A N K V E
A E T O N H T F I F E W E U
E U X J K K U M O H A T L A
M E T S I A M I Z N J A O F
```

KATSE	MOKHOLUTSOA
KHOLALA	TWEBA
KHOMO	PARROT
NTJA	LIPOU
LIHLAPI	PUNYANA
LIJO	MUTLANYANA
PHOKODI	MOHATLA
HAMSTER	KGOKA
KEKETSENG	NGAKA KHOOANE
LESHA	METSI

97 - Jazz

```
X J K P M O E K E T S I Z M
S E O H T O M O H T O M M K
M X Q E K A N O B Z S U O X
M O Y L L H Q S U L T B H H
V O K A M H A I G I A L L P
G N F H X K H L N T H A A O
F I D U O L C E E E T Z P T
G M P A T A O S S B N T I A
K M K G H A M T T O O U M L
O K E S T R A Q E H H M V E
K H L Y B P H T K O K E W T
M E R W X I J N E B Y L S E
W I S I T A H T I L Z O N R
M O T S A M A I L D U C P K
```

ALBUM
LITEBOHO
MOHLAPI
MOTSAMAI
KHONTHATSO
LIEKETSENG
TS'ELISO
TUMELO
LITHATISI
MOFUTA

MMINO
MOCHA
KHALE
OKESTRA
MOTHO MOTHO
PHELA
MOKHOA
TALETE
MOEKETSI

98 - Nature

```
M O H L O M I P A J M P L L
K O S Y T O S I L E S T E E
W H E M A L Z V H L W K H F
R A O K G O V G E T X H L E
S C X T F F Y N M N B O A E
D Y E F S O Z E C O O H K L
S U E V Q O G B P B H O E A
O E B V E H Q A H A L H L S
H G R Z R P T H N H O O A J
S T A E V I X T U E K A N B
M A R U N L E I Š T O N I L
J O K F C E J L O P A L O M
T Š E B E L E T S O G L B V
A R C T I C K H A H L I S A
```

LIPHOOFOLO
ARCTIC
BONTLE
LINOTŠI
MARU
LEFEELA
MOHLOMI
KHOHOHOA
FOGANE
LEHLAKELA

MEHLA
KHAHLISA
LITHABENG
KHOTSO
MOLAPO
TS'ELISO
SERENE
TŠEBELETSO
BOHLOKOA
HLAHA

99 - Vacation #2

```
C J M O Š T N A O Š T I L W
L W C O S I L E S T I S E C
E E L E T O H S S B E E B U
E M V C G S I Y U S H K O H
T M G N E B A H T I L E T N
O C A T P D L M M O P T E L
F X J P H U W P A Y H T N E
U H E Y L U F P F I O E G B
T S A M A I T R O T M N N A
P A S E K A D O F A O T J K
X O I T A G M S E R L E E A
I C V V F M G L S A O N M I
S E H L A K A N E R V G J Y
L E O A T L A B A H C O M F
```

SEFOFA

LEBOTENG

MOTSAMAI

LEBAKA

MOCHABA

PHOMOLO

HOTELE

SEHLAKANE

LEETO

TS'ELISO

MAP

LITHABENG

PASEKA

LITŠOANTŠO

LEOATLA

TEKESI

TENTENG

THUTO

TSAMAI

VISA

100 - Electricity

```
Y  S  X  K  M  Y  L  I  E  K  E  T  S  O
L  Z  E  M  L  O  P  O  H  K  I  L  X  H
A  E  O  B  Y  K  H  D  A  W  T  N  U  F
S  N  S  V  E  O  T  A  H  T  E  B  E  L
E  O  T  I  A  L  B  P  U  R  K  P  E  I
R  S  E  E  P  O  I  G  R  U  P  W  R  Q
L  T  L  M  M  P  S  S  M  P  A  W  D  N
M  E  E  W  T  V  T  T  A  S  K  A  O  N
O  L  B  H  B  B  A  M  A  G  N  E  T  E
H  E  E  O  P  U  L  K  H  A  B  A  N  E
L  B  Š  Q  N  W  T  L  D  T  P  X  S  Y
O  E  T  Y  A  A  O  S  O  K  E  T  E  J
M  Š  R  V  B  Y  M  M  R  H  V  F  L  B
I  T  M  O  E  K  E  T  S  I  O  M  E  T
```

LEBETHA	MAGNETE
KHABANE	TŠEBELETSO
MOTLATSI	LIEKETSO
MOEKETSI	SOKETE
SEBELISA	POLOKO
MOHLOMI	MOHAU
LEBONA	TŠEBELETSOE
LASER	LIKHOPO

1 - Antiques

2 - Food #1

3 - Measurements

4 - Farm #2

5 - Books

6 - Meditation

7 - Days and Months

8 - Energy

9 - Archeology

10 - Food #2

11 - Chemistry

12 - Music

13 - Family

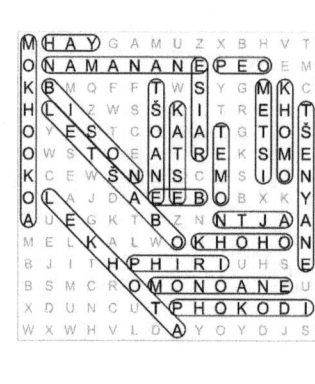

14 - Farm #1

15 - Camping

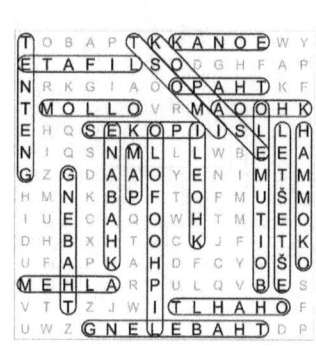

16 - Algebra

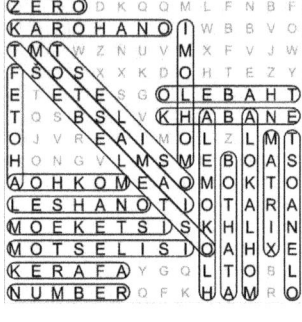

17 - Spices

18 - Universe

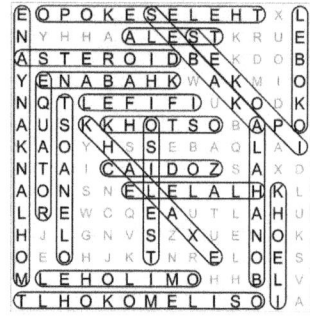

19 - Mammals

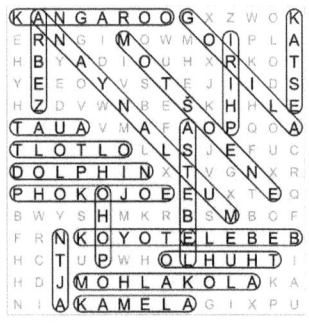

20 - Fishing

21 - Restaurant #1

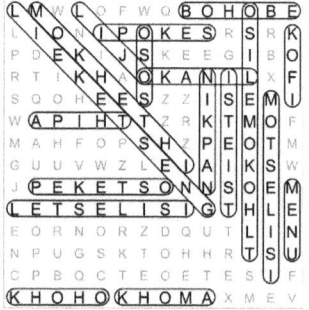

22 - Bees

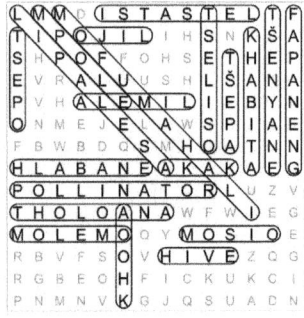

23 - Weather

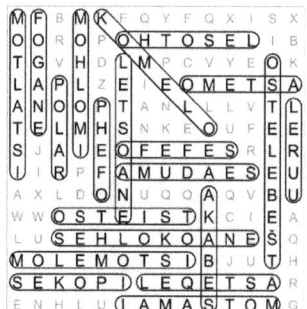

24 - Adventure

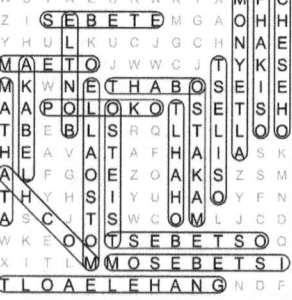

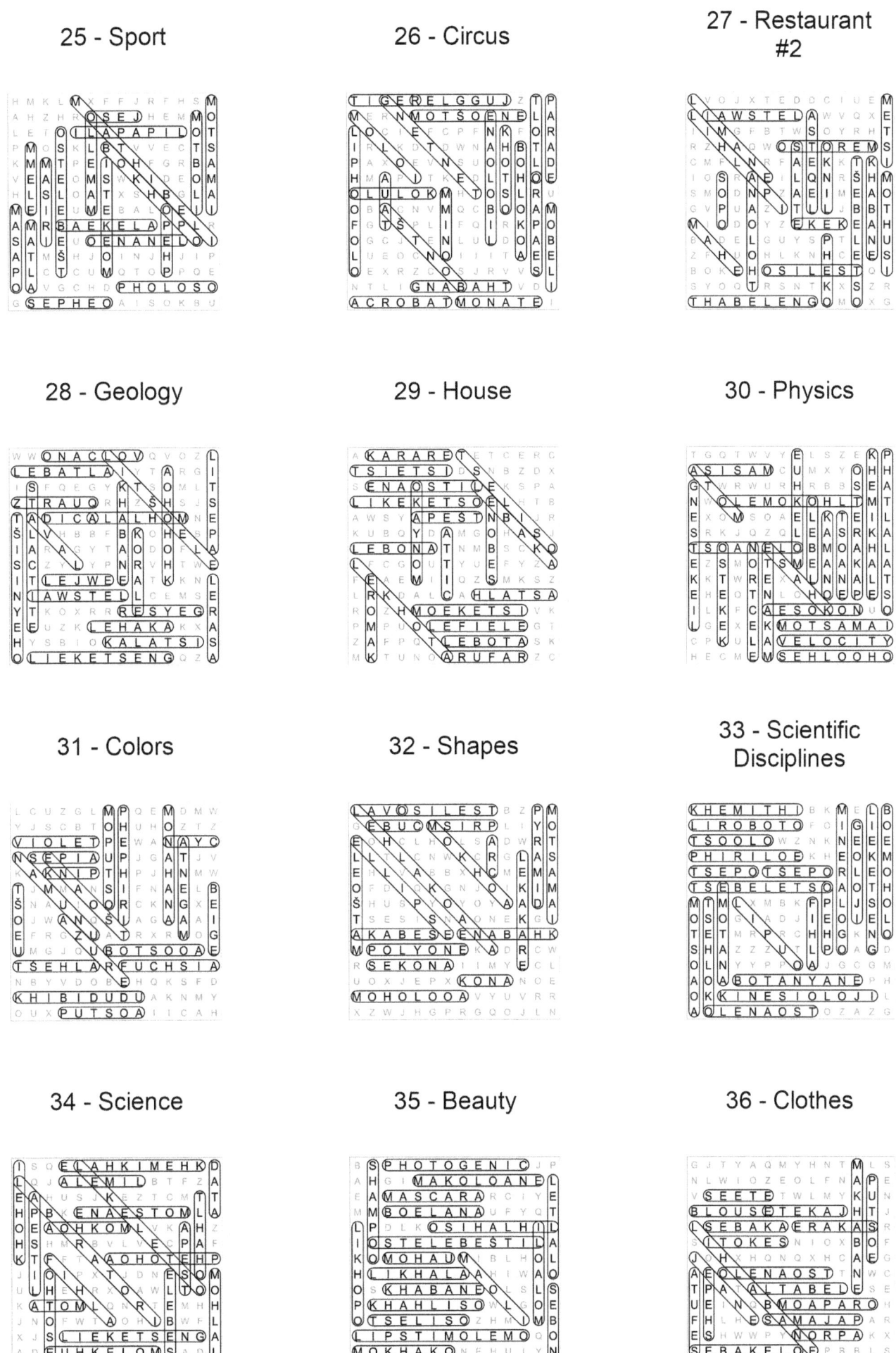

25 - Sport

26 - Circus

27 - Restaurant #2

28 - Geology

29 - House

30 - Physics

31 - Colors

32 - Shapes

33 - Scientific Disciplines

34 - Science

35 - Beauty

36 - Clothes

37 - Insects

38 - Astronomy

39 - Health and Wellness #2

40 - Time

41 - Buildings

42 - Gardening

43 - Herbalism

44 - Vehicles

45 - Flowers

46 - Health and Wellness #1

47 - Town

48 - Antarctica

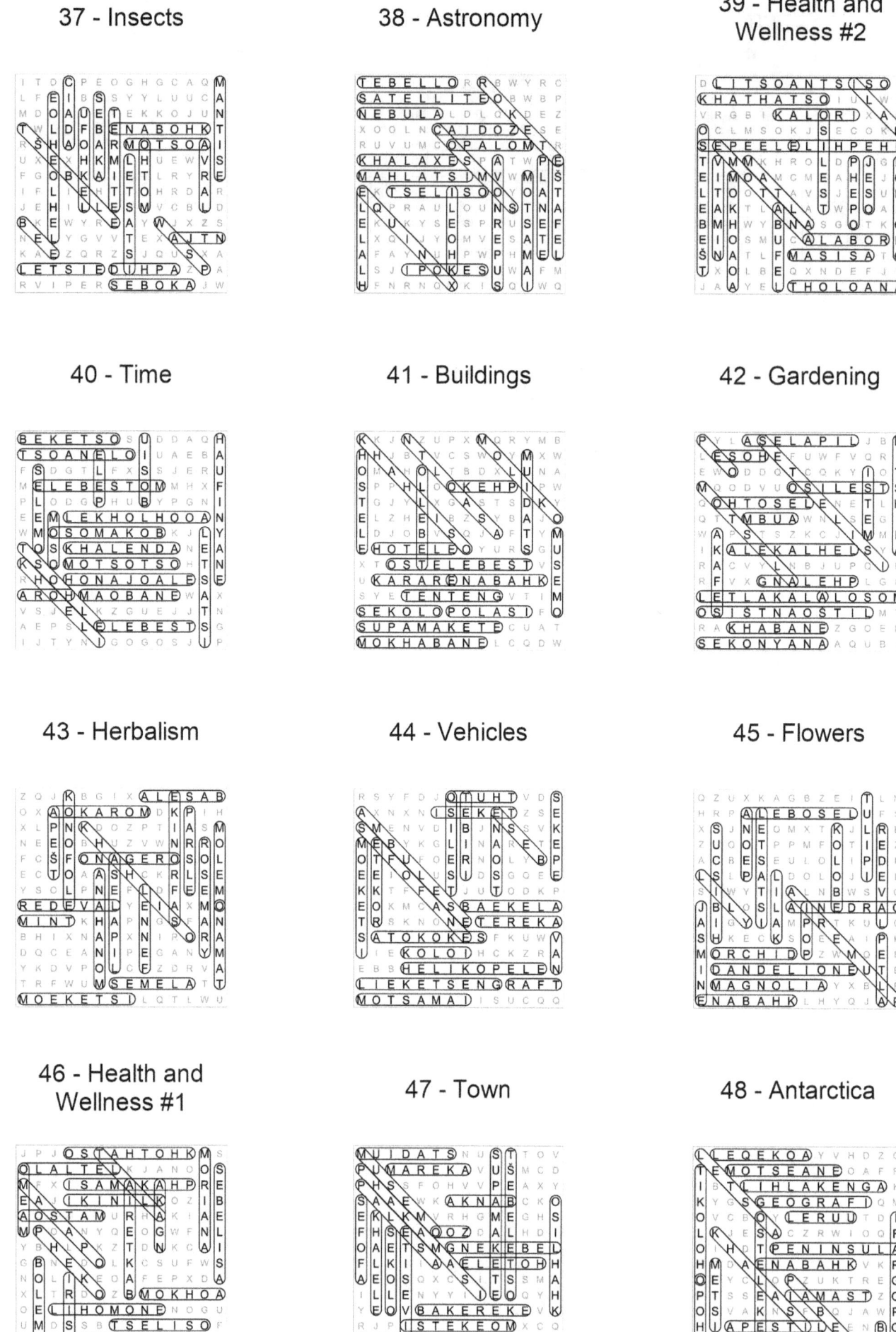

49 - Ballet

50 - Fashion

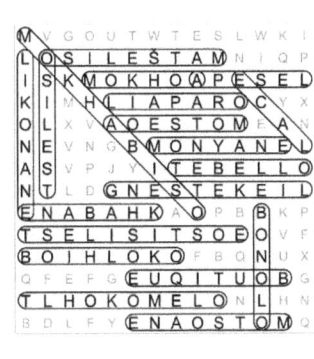

51 - Human Body

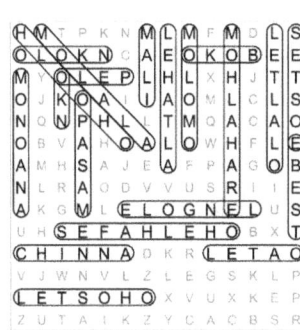

52 - Musical Instruments

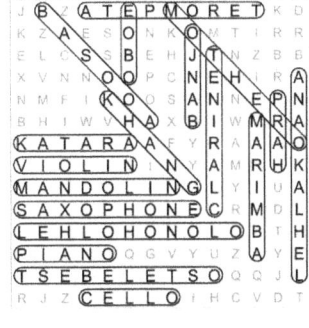

53 - Fruit

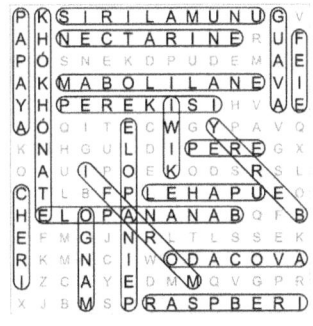

54 - Engineering

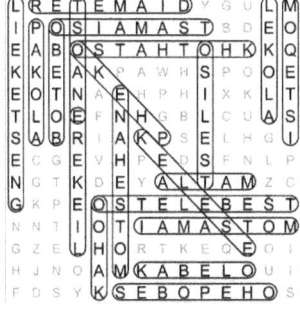

55 - Kitchen

56 - Government

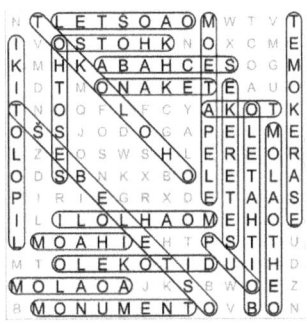

57 - Art Supplies

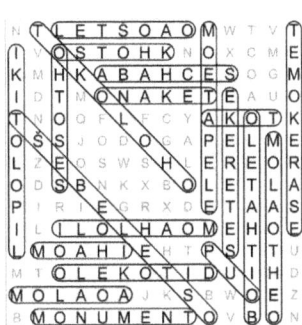

58 - Science Fiction

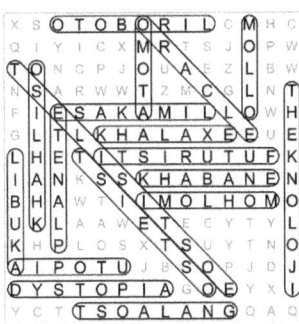

59 - Geometry

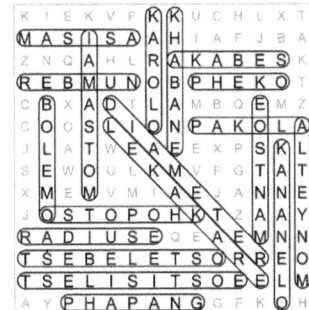

60 - Airplanes

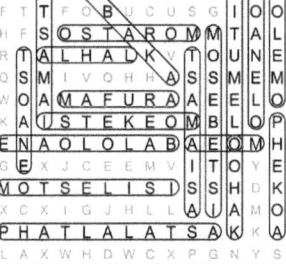

61 - Ocean

62 - Force and Gravity

63 - Birds

64 - Nutrition

65 - Hiking

66 - Professions #1

67 - Barbecues

68 - Chocolate

69 - Vegetables

70 - Boats

71 - Driving

72 - Professions #2

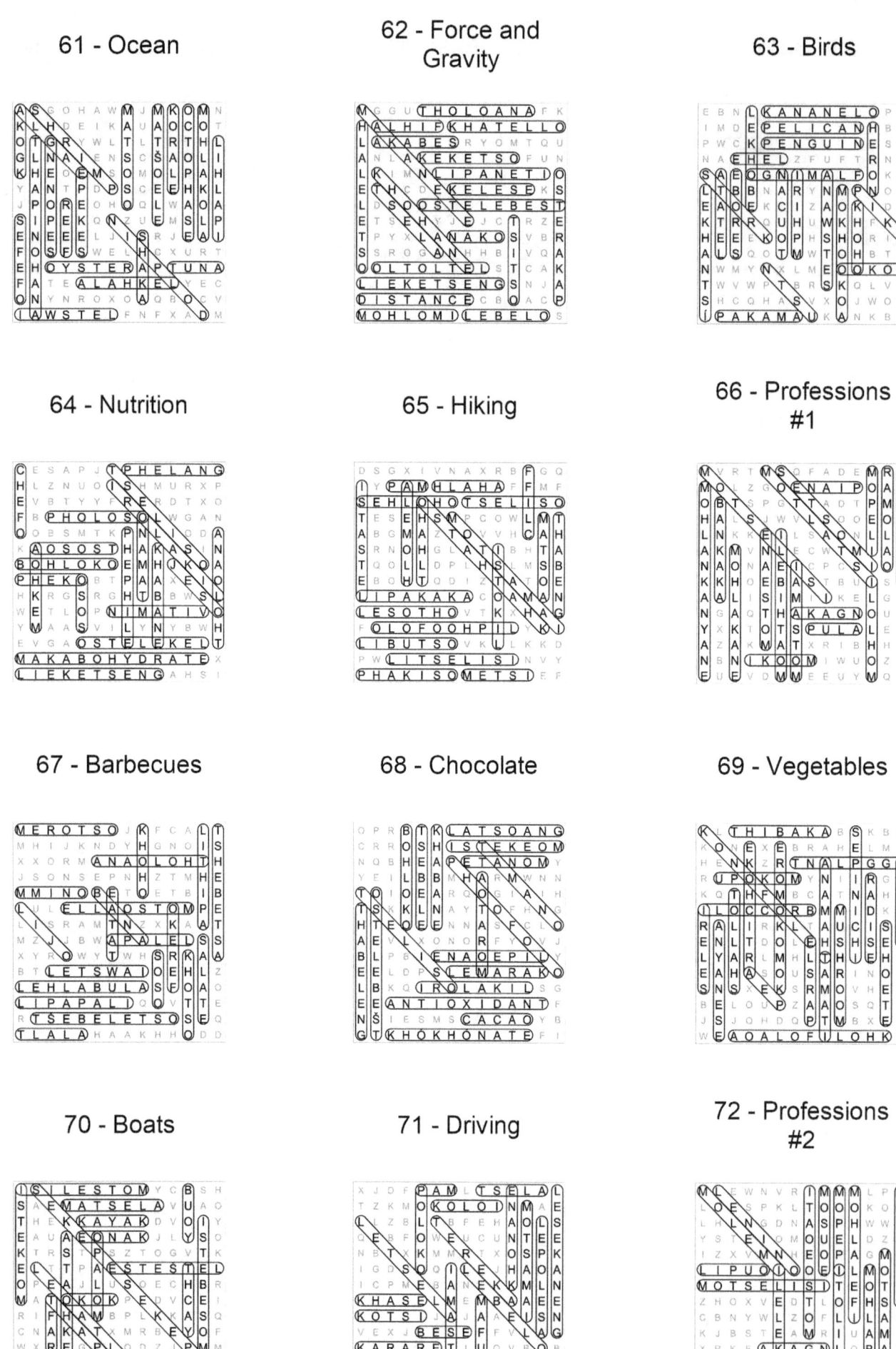

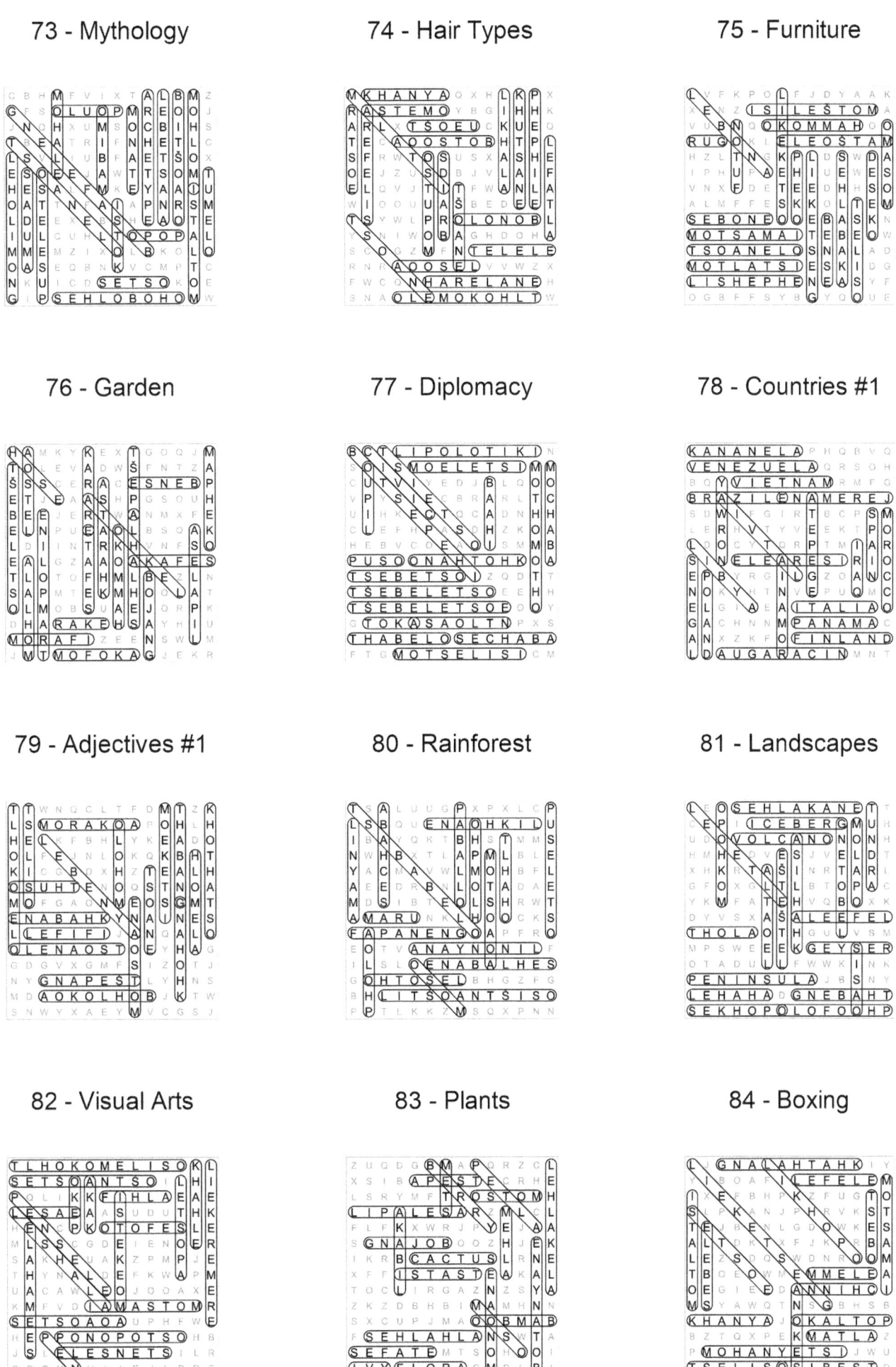

73 - Mythology

74 - Hair Types

75 - Furniture

76 - Garden

77 - Diplomacy

78 - Countries #1

79 - Adjectives #1

80 - Rainforest

81 - Landscapes

82 - Visual Arts

83 - Plants

84 - Boxing

85 - Countries #2

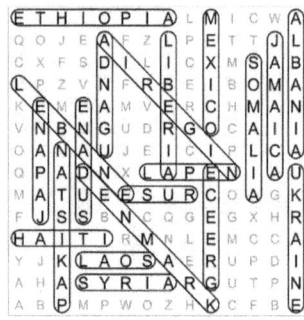

86 - Ecology

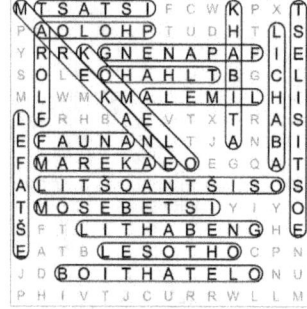

87 - Adjectives #2

88 - Psychology

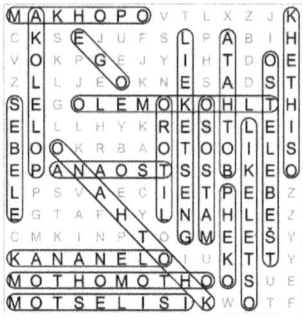

89 - Math

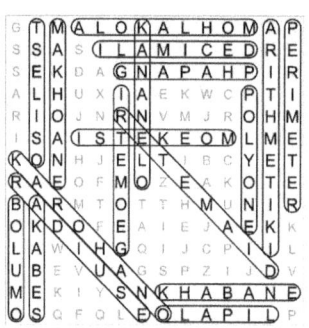

90 - Water

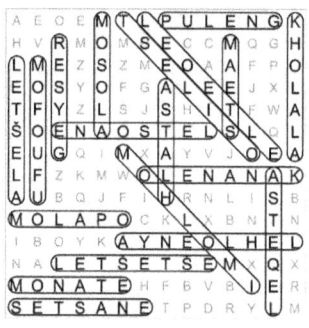

91 - Activities

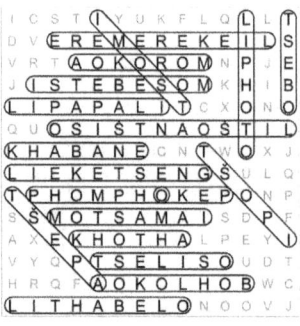

92 - Business

93 - The Company

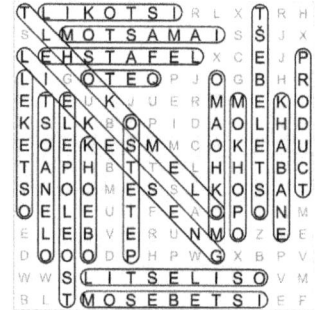

94 - Literature

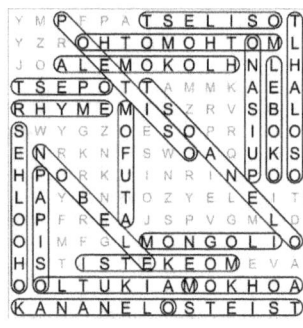

95 - Geography

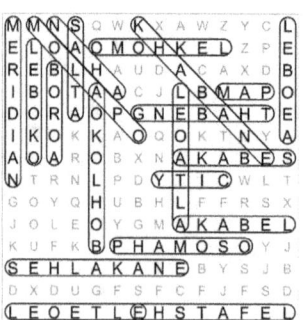

96 - Pets

97 - Jazz

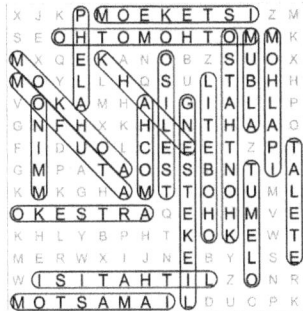

98 - Nature

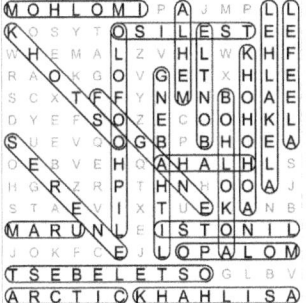

99 - Vacation #2

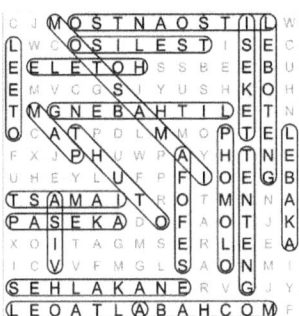

100 - Electricity

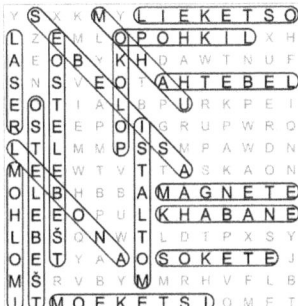

Dictionary

Activities
Mesebetsi

Activity	Mosebetsi
Art	Litšoantšiso
Camping	Motsamai
Ceramics	Liekeremere
Crafts	Lieketseng
Fishing	Tšopi
Games	Lipapali
Gardening	Tšepa
Hunting	Tsomi
Interests	Lithabelo
Knitting	Khotha
Leisure	Ts'Eliso
Magic	Bohlokoa
Painting	Peko
Photography	Liphoto
Pleasure	Thabelo
Reading	Khabane
Relaxation	Phompho
Sewing	Morokoa
Skill	Tsebo

Adjectives #1
Maemedi #1

Absolute	Khothatso
Ambitious	Khabane
Aromatic	Morakoa
Artistic	Moeketsi
Attractive	Khohang
Beautiful	Khabane
Dark	Lefifi
Exotic	Ts'Eliso
Generous	Khabane
Happy	Thabang
Heavy	Hlomela
Helpful	Thuso
Honest	Tšepang
Huge	Moholo
Identical	Ts'Oanelo
Modern	Mots'Oane
Serious	Tlhokomelo
Slow	Lebenya
Thin	Ts'Oane
Valuable	Bohlokoa

Adjectives #2
Maemedi #2

Authentic	Tšebeletso
Creative	Mokhopo
Descriptive	Hlalosi
Dry	Ometsa
Elegant	Khabane
Famous	Tumelo
Gifted	Limpho
Healthy	Phephile
Hot	Tshebetsa
Hungry	Tlala
Interesting	Thabang
Natural	Tlhaho
New	Mocha
Productive	Hlalisa
Proud	Khanya
Responsible	Boikabelo
Salty	Letswai
Sleepy	Robala
Strong	Matlatsa
Wild	Hlaha

Adventure
Boithabiso

Activity	Mosebetsi
Beauty	Bontle
Bravery	Sebete
Challenges	Mathata
Chance	Monyetla
Dangerous	Tsietso
Destination	Lebaka
Enthusiasm	Cheseho
Excursion	Ts'Eliso
Friends	Motsoalle
Itinerary	Ts'Ebetso
Joy	Thabo
Nature	Tlhaho
New	Mocha
Preparation	Phakiso
Safety	Poloko
Surprising	Makatso
Travels	Maeto
Unusual	Tloaelehang

Airplanes
Lifofane

Adventure	Boitumelo
Air	Moea
Altitude	Phekoa
Atmosphere	Sebaka
Balloon	Baloloane
Construction	Kahoo
Crew	Mosebetsi
Descent	Ts'Eliso
Design	Moratso
Engine	Ts'Oane
Fuel	Mafura
Height	Bolemo
History	Ts'Oanelo
Inflate	Phatlalatsa
Landing	Lahla
Navigate	Tsamaisa
Passenger	Moeketsi
Pilot	Motsamai
Sky	Sekopi
Turbulence	Mots'Elisi

Algebra
Algebra

Diagram	Tšebeletso
Division	Karohano
Equation	Khabane
Exponent	Mohlakola
Factor	Ts'Oanelo
False	Leshano
Formula	Motsamai
Fraction	Moeketsi
Graph	Kerafa
Infinite	Mohlomi
Linear	Mokhoa
Matrix	Matrix
Number	Number
Parenthesis	Mots'Elisi
Problem	Bothata
Simplify	Hlokomela
Solution	Thabelo
Subtraction	Ts'Eliso
Variable	Fetoha
Zero	Zero

Antarctica
Antarctica

Bay	Bay
Birds	Linonyana
Clouds	Leruu
Conservation	Pabelo
Continent	Khabane
Cove	Khopo
Environment	Tikoloho
Expedition	Lekeletso
Geography	Geografi
Glaciers	Khalasi
Ice	Leqekoa
Islands	Lihlakenga
Migration	Tsamai
Minerals	Lits'Epa
Peninsula	Peninsula
Researcher	Moeketsi
Rocky	Lets'Oa
Scientific	Mots'Eane
Topography	Topografi
Water	Metsi

Antiques
Lintho tsa Khale

Art	Litšoantšiso
Auction	Thekiso
Authentic	Tšebeletso
Century	Lekholhooa
Coins	Lits'Eliso
Collector	Moeketsi
Decades	Lilemo
Decorative	Mokhabiso
Furniture	Ts'Eliso
Gallery	Khalele
Investment	Petetso
Jewelry	Makhabane
Old	Khale
Price	Theko
Quality	Khabane
Restoration	Puseletso
Sculpture	Sets'Oaoa
Style	Mokhoa
Unusual	Tloaelehang
Value	Value

Archeology
Boepolli ba Lintho tsa K

Analysis	Ts'Eliso
Antiquity	Mokhale-Khale
Bones	Masapo
Civilization	Ts'Oetsoe
Era	Era
Expert	Setsebi
Forgotten	Lebelang
Fossil	Mohlala
Fragments	Lieketsana
Mystery	Semphiri
Objects	Lieketso
Professor	Motsamai
Relic	Relek
Researcher	Moeketsi
Team	Team
Temple	Tempele
Tomb	Lebitla
Unknown	Tsebang
Years	Lilemo

Art Supplies
Lisebelisoa tsa Art

Acrylic	Acrylic
Brushes	Litšoane
Camera	Kakamera
Chair	Ts'Eliso
Charcoal	Leshala
Clay	Letsopa
Colors	Makala
Creativity	Tlhokomeliso
Easel	Easel
Eraser	Raser
Glue	Sekhopotso
Ideas	Makhopo
Ink	Enka
Oil	Oli
Paper	Pampiri
Pastels	Pasele
Pencils	Lipenyane
Table	Tafole
Water	Metsi

Astronomy
Thuto ea Linaleli

Asteroid	Asteroid
Astronaut	Motsamai
Astronomer	Mohlankanyane
Constellation	Ts'Eliso
Cosmos	Cosmos
Earth	Lefatše
Equinox	Equinox
Galaxy	Khalaxe
Meteor	Molapo
Moon	Khoeli
Nebula	Nebula
Observatory	Tebello
Planet	Planete
Radiation	Mahlatsi
Rocket	Rokete
Satellite	Satellite
Sky	Sekopi
Solar	Hlalele
Supernova	Supernova
Zodiac	Zodiac

Ballet
Ballet

Applause	Liteboho
Audience	Batheeletsi
Choreography	Choreografi
Composer	Mohlapi
Dancers	Batlisisi
Expressive	Tšoeletso
Gesture	Ts'Itso
Graceful	Mohau
Intensity	Khothatso
Muscles	Masiri
Music	Mmino
Orchestra	Okestra
Practice	Ts'Eliso
Rehearsal	Ts'Oetsoe
Rhythm	Motho Motho
Skill	Tsebo
Style	Mokhoa
Technique	Moeketsi

Barbecues
Li-Barbecue

Chicken	Khoho
Children	Bana
Dinner	Tšebeletso
Family	Lelapa
Food	Lijo
Forks	Fereko
Friends	Motsoalle
Fruit	Tholoana
Games	Lipapali
Grill	Khotso
Hot	Tshebetsa
Hunger	Tlala
Knives	Lithipa
Music	Mmino
Salads	Salate
Salt	Letswai
Sauce	Soso
Summer	Lehlabula
Tomatoes	Tatae
Vegetables	Merotso

Beauty
Botle

Charm	Khahliso
Color	Molaoli
Cosmetics	Likhopo
Curls	Likhala
Elegant	Khabane
Fragrance	Mokhako
Grace	Mohau
Lipstick	Lipsti Molemo
Makeup	Boelana
Mascara	Mascara
Mirror	Sebone
Oils	Maoli
Photogenic	Photogenic
Products	Lihlahiso
Scent	Makoloane
Scissors	Sekelesi
Services	Litšebeletso
Shampoo	Shampoo
Skin	Letlalo
Stylist	Ts'Eliso

Bees
Linotsi

Beneficial	Molemo
Blossom	Ts'Eliso
Diversity	Fapaneng
Ecosystem	Ts'Epo
Flowers	Lipalesa
Food	Lijo
Fruit	Tholoana
Garden	Tšepa
Habitat	Khabita
Hive	Hive
Honey	Tšenyane
Insect	Khooa
Plants	Limela
Pollen	Mpole
Pollinator	Pollinator
Queen	Mofumahali
Smoke	Mosio
Sun	Letsatsi
Swarm	Hlabane
Wax	Kaka

Birds
Linonyana

Canary	Kananelo
Chicken	Khoho
Crow	Mokhookoa
Cuckoo	Kokoo
Duck	Letata
Eagle	Ntsu
Egg	Lehe
Flamingo	Flamingo
Goose	Lekhantsí
Gull	Lekhobe
Heron	Heron
Ostrich	Mphiri
Parrot	Pakama
Peacock	Piko
Pelican	Pelican
Penguin	Penguin
Sparrow	Serobe
Stork	Stork
Swan	Setswana
Toucan	Toucan

Boats
Likepe

Anchor	Lekhotla
Buoy	Buoy
Canoe	Kanoe
Crew	Mosebetsi
Dock	Koko
Engine	Ts'Oane
Ferry	Moeketsi
Kayak	Kayak
Lake	Letšetše
Mast	Matsela
Nautical	Natholi
Ocean	Leoetle
Raft	Raft
River	Molapo
Rope	Thapo
Sailboat	Sekepe Sekepe
Sailor	Mots'Elisi
Sea	Leoatla
Tide	Lekhoatsa
Yacht	Yacht

Books
Libuka

Adventure	Boitumelo
Author	Mongoli
Collection	Bokolo
Context	Tebello
Duality	Khabane
Epic	Epic
Historical	Ts'Oanelo
Humorous	Tšebeletso
Literary	Moleleki
Novel	Nobele
Page	Leqephe
Poem	Leboko
Poetry	Potso
Reader	Moeketsi
Relevant	Tlhokomelo
Series	Lehlokoa
Story	Pale
Tragic	Bohloko
Words	Mantsoe
Written	Kholoa

Boxing
Papali ea Litebele

Bell	Sebele
Body	Mmele
Chin	Chinna
Corner	Sek'Ona
Elbow	Sets'Oe
Exhausted	Khathalang
Fighter	Motsamai
Fist	Lefele
Focus	Tsebiso
Gloves	Litšoane
Kick	Khanya
Opponent	Mohanyetsi
Points	Lieketseng
Quick	Potlako
Recovery	Ts'Eliso
Referee	Motlatsi
Ropes	Likhopo
Skill	Tsebo
Strength	Matla

Buildings
Mehaho

Apartment	Pheko
Barn	Moliko
Cabin	Khabane
Cinema	Khahliso
Embassy	Ntloasa
Factory	Mokhabane
Farm	Polasi
Garage	Karare
Hospital	Sepeele
Hostel	Hostele
Hotel	Hotele
Laboratory	Laboratori
Museum	Musemo
School	Sekolo
Stadium	Stadium
Supermarket	Supamakete
Tent	Tenteng
Theater	Tšebeletso
Tower	Tebello
University	Univesite

Business
Khoebo

Boss	Mokhosi
Budget	Tebello
Company	Kopane
Cost	Litšeko
Discount	Theko
Economics	Motlotlo
Employee	Mosebetsi
Employer	Mohiri
Factory	Mokhabane
Income	Letseno
Investment	Petetso
Manager	Molaoli
Merchandise	Mothoabi
Money	Chelete
Office	Ofisi
Profit	Molemo
Sale	Thekiso
Shop	Lebekeng
Taxes	Lekhetho
Transaction	Tšebeletso

Camping
Ho Kampa

Adventure	Boitumelo
Animals	Liphoofolo
Cabin	Khabane
Canoe	Kanoe
Compass	Kopase
Fire	Mollo
Forest	Mehla
Fun	Thabeleng
Hammock	Hammoko
Hat	Sekopi
Hunting	Tsomi
Insect	Khooa
Lake	Letšetše
Map	Map
Moon	Khoeli
Mountain	Thabeng
Nature	Tlhaho
Rope	Thapo
Tent	Tenteng
Trees	Lifate

Chemistry
Khemistri

Acid	Acid
Alkaline	Alkaline
Atomic	Atomo
Carbon	Khabane
Catalyst	Ts'Eliso
Chlorine	Chlorine
Electron	Electron
Enzyme	Ennyme
Gas	Khase
Heat	Mocheso
Hydrogen	Moeketsi
Ion	Ion
Liquid	Moqetsi
Metals	Litšepe
Molecule	Molek'Hue
Nuclear	Nokosea
Organic	Ts'Epa
Oxygen	Oksense
Salt	Letswai
Weight	Tholoana

Chocolate
Tsokolate

Antioxidant	Antioxidant
Bitter	Bohloko
Cacao	Cacao
Calories	Likalori
Caramel	Karamel
Coconut	Khókhónate
Delicious	Thabeleng
Exotic	Ts'Eliso
Favorite	Moratoa
Flavor	Tamano
Ingredient	Moeketsi
Peanuts	Lipeoane
Powder	Phoofolo
Quality	Khabane
Recipe	Tšebeletso
Sugar	Ts'Ebele
Sweet	Monate
Taste	Latsoang

Circus
Circus

Acrobat	Acrobat
Animals	Liphoofolo
Balloons	Liboloane
Candy	Monate
Clown	Kolulo
Costume	Seaparo
Elephant	Tlotlo
Entertain	Thabang
Juggler	Juggler
Lion	Taua
Magic	Bohlokoa
Magician	Moloi
Monkey	Motšoene
Music	Mmino
Parade	Parade
Show	Bontša
Spectator	Mobeli
Tent	Tenteng
Tiger	Tiger
Trick	Khotso

Clothes
Liaparo

Apron	Apron
Belt	Lebatla
Blouse	Blouse
Bracelet	Sebaka
Coat	Sebakelo
Dress	Moaparo
Fashion	Ts'Oanelo
Gloves	Litšoane
Hat	Sekopi
Jacket	Jakete
Jeans	Jeane
Jewelry	Makhabane
Pajamas	Pajamas
Pants	Putsoe
Sandals	Lihlabane
Scarf	Sakare
Shirt	Shepe
Shoe	Seete
Skirt	Sekoti
Sweater	Sefuta

Colors
Mebala

Azure	Azure
Beige	Beige
Black	Tšoane
Blue	Putsoa
Brown	Botsooa
Cyan	Cyan
Fuchsia	Fuchsia
Green	Monahana
Grey	Moputso
Magenta	Magenta
Orange	Namunu
Pink	Pink
Purple	Phephiri
Red	Khibidudu
Sepia	Sepia
Violet	Violet
White	Tšoeu
Yellow	Tšehla

Countries #1
Linaha #1

Brazil	Brazile
Canada	Kananela
Egypt	Egepeta
Finland	Finland
Germany	Jeremane
Iraq	Iraq
Israel	Iseraele
Italy	Italia
Latvia	Latvia
Libya	Libya
Morocco	Morocco
Nicaragua	Nicaragua
Norway	Norway
Panama	Panama
Poland	Poland
Romania	Romania
Senegal	Senegal
Spain	Spain
Venezuela	Venezuela
Vietnam	Vietnam

Countries #2
Linaha #2

Albania	Albania
Denmark	Denmark
Ethiopia	Ethiopia
Greece	Greece
Haiti	Haiti
Jamaica	Jamaica
Japan	Japane
Laos	Laos
Lebanon	Lebane
Liberia	Liberia
Mexico	Mexico
Nepal	Nepal
Nigeria	Nigeria
Pakistan	Pakistan
Russia	Ruse
Somalia	Somalia
Sudan	Sudane
Syria	Syria
Uganda	Uganda
Ukraine	Ukraine

Days and Months
Matsatsi le Likhoeli

April	April
August	Phakane
Calendar	Khalenda
February	Hlakola
Friday	Khetha
January	Phekoane
July	Phuptjane
March	Marekane
May	May
Monday	Mosotho
Month	Khoeli
November	Tšoanelo
October	Mphato
Saturday	Moqehlo
September	Tšepane
Sunday	Khabane
Thursday	Ts'Eliso
Week	Beketso
Year	Selemo

Diplomacy
Didiplomate

Adviser	Moeletsi
Ambassador	Mots'Elisi
Citizens	Baahi
Civic	Civic
Community	Sechaba
Conflict	Khothano
Cooperation	Ts'Ebetso
Diplomatic	Tšebeletsoe
Discussion	Tšebeletso
Embassy	Ntloasa
Foreign	Mochaba
Government	Puso
Humanitarian	Motho Motho
Integrity	Bots'Epehi
Justice	Toka
Languages	Lipuo
Politics	Lipolotiki
Resolution	Tsietso
Security	Ts'Ireletso
Solution	Thabelo

Driving
Ho Kganna

Brakes	Matšoele
Bus	Bese
Car	Koloi
Danger	Kotsi
Fuel	Mafura
Garage	Karare
Gas	Khase
License	Lesekaneng
Map	Map
Motor	Motsamai
Motorcycle	Sethuuthu
Pedestrian	Motsamai
Police	Lepolesa
Road	Tsela
Safety	Poloko
Speed	Lebelo
Street	Letsela
Traffic	Tsamai
Truck	Tereka
Tunnel	Khonane

Ecology
Ecology

Climate	Lesotho
Communities	Lichaba
Diversity	Fapaneng
Drought	Komelo
Fauna	Fauna
Flora	Flora
Global	Lefatše
Habitat	Khabita
Marine	Marekane
Marsh	Mareka
Mountains	Lithabeng
Nature	Tlhaho
Plants	Limela
Resources	Mosebetsi
Species	Litšoantšiso
Survival	Pholoa
Sustainable	Ts'Elisitsoe
Vegetation	Tsatsi
Volunteers	Boithatelo

Electricity
Motlakase

Battery	Lebetha
Cable	Khabane
Electric	Motlatsi
Electrician	Moeketsi
Equipment	Sebelisa
Generator	Mohlomi
Lamp	Lebona
Laser	Laser
Magnet	Magnete
Negative	Khabane
Network	Tšebeletso
Objects	Lieketso
Positive	Khabane
Socket	Sokete
Storage	Poloko
Telephone	Mohau
Television	Tšebeletsoe
Wires	Likhopo

Energy
Matla

Battery	Lebetha
Carbon	Khabane
Diesel	Ts'Eliso
Electric	Motlatsi
Electron	Electron
Engine	Ts'Oane
Entropy	Khethiso
Environment	Tikoloho
Fuel	Mafura
Gasoline	Gasoline
Heat	Mocheso
Hydrogen	Moeketsi
Industry	Indakane
Nuclear	Nokosea
Photon	Photo
Pollution	Tšilafalo
Steam	Steam
Sun	Letsatsi
Turbine	Motsamai
Wind	Phefo

Engineering
Boenjiniere

Angle	Pheko
Axis	Kelese
Calculation	Pakola
Construction	Kahoo
Depth	Botebo
Diagram	Tšebeletso
Diameter	Diameter
Diesel	Ts'Eliso
Distribution	Kabelo
Energy	Matla
Engine	Ts'Oane
Gears	Liekere
Levers	Lieketseng
Liquid	Moqetsi
Machine	Mots'Ehane
Measurement	Lekola
Motor	Motsamai
Propulsion	Khothatso
Stability	Tsamaiso
Structure	Sebopeho

Family
Lelapa

Ancestor	Ntloli
Aunt	Mohlakane
Brother	Mokhabane
Child	Ngoana
Childhood	Ts'Oana
Children	Bana
Daughter	Ts'Oane
Father	Ntate
Grandchild	Ntloana
Grandfather	Ntloholo
Grandson	Ts'Olo
Husband	Monna
Maternal	Mots'Eli
Mother	Mots'Eoa
Nephew	Mochaba
Niece	Monyane
Paternal	Motsoali
Sister	Khasane
Uncle	Mats'Oane
Wife	Mosali

Farm #1
Polase #1

Agriculture	Temo
Bee	Bee
Bison	Bison
Calf	Namanane
Cat	Katse
Chicken	Khoho
Cow	Khomo
Crow	Mokhookoa
Dog	Ntja
Donkey	Tšoane
Fence	Lekhota
Fertilizer	Monoane
Field	Letšabo
Goat	Phokodi
Hay	Hay
Honey	Tšenyane
Horse	Phiri
Rice	Raise
Seeds	Peo
Water	Metsi

Farm #2
Polasi #2

Animals	Liphoofolo
Barley	Balali
Barn	Moliko
Corn	Poone
Duck	Letata
Farmer	Molemi
Food	Lijo
Fruit	Tholoana
Irrigation	Ts'Eliso
Lamb	Nku
Llama	Llama
Meadow	Mokhoaoa
Milk	Lebese
Orchard	Sefaka
Ripe	Bulutseng
Sheep	Likunyane
Shepherd	Molisa
Tractor	Tebiri
Vegetable	Moroto
Wheat	Kholo

Fashion
Feshene

Affordable	Ts'Elisitsoe
Boutique	Boutique
Buttons	Likonane
Clothing	Liaparo
Comfortable	Matšeliso
Elegant	Khabane
Embroidery	Mokhabiso
Expensive	Tebello
Fabric	Lesepa
Lace	Lace
Measurements	Lieketseng
Minimalist	Monyane
Modern	Mots'Oane
Modest	Boihloko
Original	Ts'Eliso
Pattern	Mots'Eoa
Simple	Bonolo
Style	Mokhoa
Texture	Tlhokomelo

Fishing
Ho Tšoasa Litlhapi

Bait	Bait
Basket	Baseka
Beach	Leboteng
Boat	Sekepe
Cook	Phehetsa
Equipment	Sebelisa
Exaggeration	Phetemello
Fins	Maphele
Gills	Lieketseng
Hook	Hokane
Jaw	Mohlahare
Lake	Letšetše
Ocean	Leoetle
Patience	Mamello
River	Molapo
Season	Sekoa
Water	Metsi
Weight	Tholoana
Wire	Khopo

Flowers
Lipalesa

Bouquet	Khabane
Clover	Kolobe
Daisy	Letsatsi
Dandelion	Dandelione
Gardenia	Gardenia
Hibiscus	Hibiscus
Jasmine	Jasmine
Lavender	Laveder
Lilac	Lilak
Lily	Lily
Magnolia	Magnolia
Orchid	Orchid
Peony	Peona
Petal	Petla
Plumeria	Plumeria
Poppy	Popi
Sunflower	Lesobela
Tulip	Tulipi

Food #1
Lijo #1

Apricot	Mabolilane
Barley	Balali
Basil	Basela
Carrot	Sehoete
Cinnamon	Kinamo
Garlic	Konofole
Juice	Maseko
Lemon	Sirilamunu
Milk	Lebese
Onion	Anyanese
Peanut	Lekoane
Pear	Pere
Salad	Salate
Salt	Letswai
Soup	Sopo
Spinach	Sepinichi
Strawberry	Strawberry
Sugar	Ts'Ebele
Tuna	Tuna
Turnip	Thibaka

Food #2
Lijo #2

Apple	Apole
Artichoke	Artichoke
Banana	Banana
Broccoli	Broccoli
Celery	Seleri
Cheese	Chese
Cherry	Cheri
Chicken	Khoho
Chocolate	Ts'Eliso
Egg	Lehe
Eggplant	Eggplant
Fish	Lihlapi
Grape	Morafi
Ham	Hemo
Kiwi	Kiwi
Mushroom	Mushroom
Rice	Raise
Tomato	Tamati
Wheat	Kholo
Yogurt	Yokote

Force and Gravity
Matla le Matla a Khoheli

Axis	Kelese
Center	Sebaka
Discovery	Hlaleletso
Distance	Distance
Dynamic	Mohlomi
Expansion	Keketso
Friction	Khohane
Impact	Tšebeletso
Magnetism	Makanete
Mechanics	Lieketseng
Motion	Ts'Itso
Orbit	Tsela
Physics	Fihla
Planets	Lipaneti
Pressure	Khatello
Properties	Letlotlo
Speed	Lebelo
Time	Nako
Universal	Pakaretso
Weight	Tholoana

Fruit
Litholoana

Apple	Apole
Apricot	Mabolilane
Avocado	Avocado
Banana	Banana
Berry	Berry
Cherry	Cheri
Coconut	Khókhónate
Fig	Feie
Grape	Morafi
Guava	Guava
Kiwi	Kiwi
Lemon	Sirilamunu
Mango	Mango
Melon	Lehapu
Nectarine	Nectarine
Papaya	Papaya
Peach	Perekisi
Pear	Pere
Pineapple	Peinapole
Raspberry	Raspberi

Furniture
Thepa ea ka Tlung

Armchair	Sehlabaka
Bed	Pheko
Bench	Bense
Bookcase	Ts'Oanelo
Chair	Ts'Eliso
Comforters	Motšelisi
Couch	Motsamai
Curtains	Likeketso
Cushions	Lieketseng
Desk	Deseko
Dresser	Motlatsi
Futon	Futon
Hammock	Hammoko
Lamp	Lebona
Mattress	Matšoele
Mirror	Sebone
Pillow	Mosamo
Rug	Rug
Shelves	Lishephe

Garden
Serapa

Bench	Bense
Bush	Sehlahla
Fence	Lekhota
Flower	Lipalesa
Garage	Karare
Garden	Tšepa
Grass	Bojang
Hammock	Hammoko
Hose	Hose
Lawn	Mohlala
Orchard	Sefaka
Pond	Lets'Oa
Porch	Mapheko
Rake	Rake
Shovel	Kharatsa
Terrace	Tšebeletso
Trampoline	Trampoline
Tree	Sefate
Vine	Morafi
Weeds	Mofoka

Gardening
Ho Lema

Bouquet	Khabane
Climate	Lesotho
Compost	Motsela
Container	Sets'Elisi
Dirt	Ditshila
Edible	Phelang
Exotic	Ts'Eliso
Floral	Lipalesa
Foliage	Lehlakela
Hose	Hose
Leaf	Letlakala
Moisture	Mosola
Orchard	Sefaka
Seasonal	Sekonyana
Seeds	Peo
Soil	Mbua
Species	Litšoantšiso
Water	Metsi

Geography
Geography

Altitude	Lekhomo
Atlas	Atlas
City	City
Country	Naha
Elevation	Phamoso
Hemisphere	Khabane
Island	Sehlakane
Latitude	Leboko
Map	Map
Meridian	Meridian
Mountain	Thabeng
North	Leboea
Ocean	Leoetle
Region	Lebaka
River	Molapo
Sea	Leoatla
South	Boroa
Territory	Sebaka
West	Bohlokoa
World	Lefatshe

Geology
Geology

Acid	Acid
Calcium	Kalatši
Cavern	Lehaka
Continent	Khabane
Coral	Korale
Crystals	Litšoele
Cycles	Lieketseng
Earthquake	Tšisinyeho
Erosion	Khohohoa
Fossil	Mohlala
Geyser	Geyser
Lava	Lava
Layer	Lerasa
Minerals	Lits'Epa
Plateau	Lebatla
Quartz	Quartz
Salt	Letswai
Stalactite	Stalactite
Stone	Lejwe
Volcano	Volcano

Geometry
Geometry

Angle	Pheko
Calculation	Pakola
Diameter	Diameter
Dimension	Tšebeletso
Equation	Khabane
Height	Bolemo
Logic	Mantsoe
Mass	Masisa
Median	Motsamai
Number	Number
Parallel	Phapang
Perpendicular	Ts'Elisitsoe
Probability	Monyetla
Proportion	Karolo
Radius	Radiuse
Square	Lekakare
Surface	Sebaka
Symmetry	Kananelo
Theory	Khopotso
Triangle	Ts'Eliso

Government
Mmuso

Citizenship	Moahi
Civil	Sesotho
Constitution	Molaotheo
Democracy	Temokerase
Discussion	Tšebeletso
District	Setereke
Equality	Tekano
Independence	Boithatelo
Judicial	Moahloli
Justice	Toka
Law	Molaoa
Leader	Moetapele
Liberty	Tokoloho
Monument	Monument
Nation	Sechaba
Peaceful	Khotso
Politics	Lipolotiki
Rights	Ditokelo
Speech	Puo
Symbol	Letšoao

Hair Types
Mefuta ea Moriri

Bald	Lefatla
Black	Tšoane
Blond	Lesooa
Braided	Ratsoe
Braids	Braids
Brown	Botsooa
Colored	Malatsi
Curls	Likhala
Curly	Harelane
Dry	Ometsa
Gray	Moputso
Healthy	Phephile
Long	Telele
Shiny	Khanya
Short	Khutsane
Silver	Silefera
Soft	Bonolo
Thin	Ts'Oane
Wavy	Tlhokomelo
White	Tšoeu

Health and Wellness #1
Bophelo bo Botle le Boph

Active	Sebelisa
Bacteria	Bakteria
Bones	Masapo
Clinic	Kliniki
Doctor	Ngaka
Fracture	Khothatso
Habit	Mokhoa
Height	Bolemo
Hormones	Lihomone
Hunger	Tlala
Injury	Ts'Eliso
Medicine	Moriana
Muscles	Masiri
Nerves	Mats'Oa
Pharmacy	Phakamasi
Posture	Maemo
Relaxation	Phompho
Skin	Letlalo
Treatment	Pheko
Virus	Vaerase

Health and Wellness #2
Bophelo bo Botle le Boph

Allergy	Tlhokomeliso
Anatomy	Anatome
Blood	Mali
Calorie	Kalori
Diet	Jeso
Disease	Lefuba
Energy	Matla
Genetics	Litšoantšiso
Healthy	Phephile
Hospital	Sepeele
Hygiene	Bohloko
Infection	Tšebeletso
Massage	Masisa
Mood	Mokhoaoa
Nutrition	Phepo
Recovery	Ts'Eliso
Sleep	Robala
Stress	Khathatso
Vitamin	Vitamin
Weight	Tholoana

Herbalism
Tšebeliso ea Litlama

Aromatic	Morakoa
Basil	Basela
Beneficial	Molemo
Culinary	Khahliso
Fennel	Fennel
Flavor	Tamano
Flower	Lipalesa
Garden	Tšepa
Garlic	Konofole
Green	Monahana
Ingredient	Moeketsi
Lavender	Laveder
Marjoram	Marjoram
Mint	Mint
Oregano	Oregano
Parsley	Parsle
Plant	Semela
Rosemary	Rosemary
Saffron	Safronike
Tarragon	Tarragon

Hiking
Ho Tsamaea ka Maoto

Animals	Liphoofolo
Boots	Libutso
Camping	Motsamai
Cliff	Cliff
Climate	Lesotho
Guides	Lits'Elisi
Hazards	Likotsi
Heavy	Hlomela
Map	Map
Mountain	Thabeng
Nature	Tlhaho
Orientation	Ts'Eliso
Parks	Lipakaka
Preparation	Phakiso
Stones	Mats'Oa
Summit	Sehloho
Sun	Letsatsi
Tired	Khathatso
Water	Metsi
Wild	Hlaha

House
Ntlo

Attic	Attic
Broom	Lefiele
Curtains	Likeketso
Door	Monyako
Fence	Lekhota
Fireplace	Sebaka Mollo
Floor	Lebaka
Furniture	Ts'Eliso
Garage	Karare
Garden	Tšepa
Keys	Lits'Oane
Kitchen	Tsietsi
Lamp	Lebona
Library	Moeketsi
Mirror	Sebone
Roof	Rafura
Room	Kamore
Shower	Hlats'A
Wall	Lebota
Window	Ts'Eliso

Human Body
'Mele oa Motho

Ankle	Nkolo
Blood	Mali
Bones	Masapo
Brain	Boko
Chin	Chinna
Ear	Tsebe
Elbow	Sets'Oe
Face	Sefahleho
Finger	Monoana
Hand	Letsoho
Head	Hlooho
Heart	Pelo
Jaw	Mohlahare
Knee	Lengole
Leg	Letao
Mouth	Molomo
Neck	Molala
Nose	Nko
Shoulder	Lehatla
Skin	Letlalo

Insects
Likokoanyana

Ant	Ntja
Aphid	Aphid
Bee	Bee
Beetle	Khobane
Butterfly	Sebaka
Cicada	Ciada
Cockroach	Lekhofu
Dragonfly	Tšebele
Flea	Letsatsi
Grasshopper	Lehloehloe
Larva	Larva
Locust	Letsie
Mantis	Mantise
Mosquito	Mots'Oa
Moth	Motho
Termite	Termite
Wasp	Wasp
Worm	Seboka

Jazz
Jazz

Album	Album
Applause	Liteboho
Composer	Mohlapi
Composition	Motsamai
Concert	Khonthatso
Drums	Lieketseng
Emphasis	Ts'Eliso
Famous	Tumelo
Favorites	Lithatisi
Genre	Mofuta
Music	Mmino
New	Mocha
Old	Khale
Orchestra	Okestra
Rhythm	Motho Motho
Song	Phela
Style	Mokhoa
Talent	Talete
Technique	Moeketsi

Kitchen
Kichine

Apron	Apron
Bowl	Sekopi
Chopsticks	Likhopo
Cups	Likobe
Food	Lijo
Forks	Fereko
Freezer	Mots'Elisi
Grill	Khahlile
Jug	Jug
Kettle	Kettle
Knives	Lithipa
Ladle	Lebaka
Napkin	Napkin
Oven	Ovane
Recipe	Tšebeletso
Refrigerator	Seitsane
Spices	Linko
Sponge	Seponeng
Spoons	Khabane

Landscapes
Libaka tsa Naha

Beach	Leboteng
Cave	Lehaha
Desert	Lefeela
Geyser	Geyser
Glacier	Khahlisa
Hill	Thola
Iceberg	Iceberg
Island	Sehlakane
Lake	Letšetše
Mountain	Thabeng
Oasis	Oasis
Ocean	Leoetle
Peninsula	Peninsula
River	Molapo
Sea	Leoatla
Swamp	Sekhopo
Tundra	Tundra
Valley	Mokhopo
Volcano	Volcano
Waterfall	Phoofolo

Literature
Lingoliloeng

Analogy	Kananelo
Analysis	Ts'Eliso
Author	Mongoli
Biography	Tšepo
Comparison	Papiso
Critique	Hlokomela
Description	Tlhaloso
Dialogue	Puisano
Fiction	Ts'Oanelo
Genre	Mofuta
Metaphor	Moeketsi
Novel	Nobele
Opinion	Maikutlo
Poem	Leboko
Poetic	Poetiso
Rhyme	Rhyme
Rhythm	Motho Motho
Style	Mokhoa
Theme	Sehlooho
Tragedy	Tsietso

Mammals
Liphoofolo tse Anyesang

Bear	Bebele
Beaver	Lebetsa
Bull	Poho
Camel	Kamela
Cat	Katse
Coyote	Koyote
Dog	Ntja
Dolphin	Dolphin
Elephant	Tlotlo
Fox	Phokojoe
Giraffe	Thuhlo
Gorilla	Gorila
Kangaroo	Kangaroo
Lion	Taua
Monkey	Motšoene
Rabbit	Mutlanyana
Sheep	Likunyane
Whale	Mohlakola
Wolf	Phiri
Zebra	Zebra

Math
Lipalo

Angles	Makhoane
Arithmetic	Arithmetiki
Decimal	Decimali
Diameter	Diameter
Division	Karohano
Equation	Khabane
Exponent	Mohlakola
Fraction	Moeketsi
Geometry	Geometri
Numbers	Lipalo
Parallel	Phapang
Perimeter	Perimeter
Perpendicular	Ts'Elisitsoe
Polygon	Polyone
Radius	Radiuse
Sphere	Sebaka
Square	Lekakare
Symmetry	Kananelo
Triangle	Ts'Eliso
Volume	Bolumo

Measurements
Litekanyo

Byte	Byte
Centimeter	Centimere
Decimal	Decimali
Degree	Lekolo
Depth	Botebo
Gram	Gram
Height	Bolemo
Inch	Inch
Kilogram	Kilomela
Kilometer	Kilometere
Length	Belele
Liter	Litere
Mass	Masisa
Meter	Metala
Minute	Motsotso
Ounce	Once
Ton	Tonana
Volume	Bolumo
Weight	Tholoana
Width	Bohlale

Meditation
Ho Thuisa

Acceptance	Kamohelo
Awake	Tsosoa
Breathing	Phefo
Calm	Tsietso
Clarity	Tlhokomelo
Compassion	Qenehelo
Emotions	Matsoso
Gratitude	Teboho
Habits	Mekhoa
Happiness	Thabo
Kindness	Mosa
Mental	Kelello
Mind	Tlhokomelo
Movement	Motsamai
Music	Mmino
Nature	Tlhaho
Observation	Tebello
Perspective	Pono Potso
Silence	Khotso
Thoughts	Likeletso

Music
Mmino

Album	Album
Ballad	Balala
Chorus	Chorus
Classical	Tšebeletso
Eclectic	Electic
Harmonic	Harmonic
Harmony	Ts'Eliso
Instrument	Sebelisa
Lyrical	Molaoli
Melody	Melodi
Microphone	Maikroofane
Musical	Minopi
Opera	Opera
Poetic	Poetiso
Recording	Tlakoa
Rhythm	Motho Motho
Rhythmic	Tšebeletsoe
Sing	Phela
Singer	Mopeli
Vocal	Tsohle

Musical Instruments
Liletsa tsa 'Mino

Banjo	Banjo
Bassoon	Basooa
Cello	Cello
Clarinet	Clarinet
Drum	Mothero
Flute	Lehlakoana
Gong	Khang
Guitar	Katara
Harp	Harp
Mandolin	Mandolin
Marimba	Marimba
Oboe	Oboe
Percussion	Lehlohonolo
Piano	Piano
Saxophone	Saxophone
Tambourine	Tambouine
Trombone	Tšebeletso
Trumpet	Terompeta
Violin	Violin

Mythology
Tšōmo

Archetype	Archetype
Behavior	Boitšoaro
Beliefs	Tumelo
Creation	Popo
Creature	Sehloboho
Culture	Setso
Deities	Mabimo
Disaster	Kotsi
Heaven	Leholimong
Hero	Mohale
Immortality	Bosafeleng
Jealousy	Poulo
Labyrinth	Lebetsana
Legend	Ts'Oanelo
Lightning	Motlatsi
Monster	Monate
Mortal	Mohlomi
Revenge	Puseletso
Thunder	Seaduma
Warrior	Mohlabane

Nature
Tlhaho

Animals	Liphoofolo
Arctic	Arctic
Beauty	Bontle
Bees	Linotši
Clouds	Maru
Desert	Lefeela
Dynamic	Mohlomi
Erosion	Khohohoa
Fog	Fogane
Foliage	Lehlakela
Forest	Mehla
Glacier	Khahlisa
Mountains	Lithabeng
Peaceful	Khotso
River	Molapo
Sanctuary	Ts'Eliso
Serene	Serene
Tropical	Tšebeletso
Vital	Bohlokoa
Wild	Hlaha

Nutrition
Phepo e Nepahetseng

Balanced	Lekeletso
Bitter	Bohloko
Calories	Likalori
Carbohydrates	Makabohydrate
Diet	Jeso
Digestion	Ts'Eliso
Edible	Phelang
Fermentation	Tsosoa
Flavor	Tamano
Habits	Mekhoa
Health	Pholoso
Healthy	Phephile
Liquids	Lieketseng
Nutrient	Pheko
Proteins	Lieketseng
Quality	Khabane
Sauce	Soso
Toxin	Chefo
Vitamin	Vitamin
Weight	Tholoana

Ocean
Leoatle

Algae	Algae
Boat	Sekepe
Coral	Korale
Crab	Lekhala
Dolphin	Dolphin
Eel	Tlhapinohana
Fish	Lihlapi
Octopus	Octophase
Oyster	Oyster
Reef	Reef
Salt	Letswai
Shark	Shaka
Shrimp	Shrimp
Sponge	Seponeng
Storm	Sefefo
Tides	Matšoele
Tuna	Tuna
Turtle	Kgoka
Waves	Matsoso
Whale	Mohlakola

Pets
Liphoofolo tse Ruuoang L

Cat	Katse
Collar	Kholala
Cow	Khomo
Dog	Ntja
Fish	Lihlapi
Food	Lijo
Goat	Phokodi
Hamster	Hamster
Kitten	Keketseng
Leash	Lesha
Lizard	Mokholutsoa
Mouse	Tweba
Parrot	Parrot
Paws	Lipou
Puppy	Punyana
Rabbit	Mutlanyana
Tail	Mohatla
Turtle	Kgoka
Veterinarian	Ngaka Khooane
Water	Metsi

Physics
Fisiks

Acceleration	Phatlalatso
Atom	Atom
Chaos	Tlhokomelo
Chemical	K'Hemik'Hale
Density	Tšoanelo
Electron	Electron
Engine	Ts'Oane
Formula	Motsamai
Frequency	Keketso
Gas	Khase
Magnetism	Makanete
Mass	Masisa
Mechanics	Lieketseng
Molecule	Molek'Hue
Nuclear	Nokosea
Particle	Sehlooho
Relativity	Kamano
Speed	Lebelo
Universal	Pakaretso
Velocity	Velocity

Plants
Limela

Bamboo	Bamboo
Bean	Libaka
Berry	Berry
Botany	Botanyane
Bush	Sehlahla
Cactus	Cactus
Fertilizer	Monoane
Flora	Flora
Flower	Lipalesa
Foliage	Lehlakela
Forest	Mehla
Garden	Tšepa
Grass	Bojang
Ivy	Ivy
Moss	Moso
Petal	Petla
Root	Motso
Stem	Stem
Tree	Sefate
Vegetation	Tsatsi

Professions #1
Litsebi #1

Ambassador	Mots'Elisi
Astronomer	Mohlankanyane
Athlete	Moathibeli
Attorney	Moeketsi
Banker	Bankaka
Coach	Moeketsi
Dancer	Motsamai
Doctor	Ngaka
Editor	Mohloli
Geologist	Motsamai
Hunter	Setsomi
Jeweler	Mohlakane
Lawyer	Ramolao
Musician	Mopeli
Nurse	Mooki
Pianist	Piane
Plumber	Pula
Scientist	Mots'Eane
Tailor	Motlatsi
Veterinarian	Ngaka Khooane

Professions #2
Litsebi #2

Astronaut	Motsamai
Chemist	Khemileng
Dentist	Lenino
Engineer	Moeketsi
Farmer	Molemi
Inventor	Mohlabi
Journalist	Mokeleli
Librarian	Mots'Elisi
Linguist	Lipuo
Painter	Mopepi
Philosopher	Mohlalefi
Photographer	Motsamai
Physician	Ngaka
Pilot	Motsamai
Politician	Moliloti
Surgeon	Tšebeletso
Teacher	Mosuoe
Zoologist	Mots'Oeoati

Psychology
Psychology

Appointment	Khethiso
Assessment	Kananelo
Behavior	Boitšoaro
Childhood	Ts'Oana
Clinical	Mots'Elisi
Cognition	Tlhokomelo
Conflict	Khothano
Dreams	Litoro
Ego	Ego
Emotions	Matsoso
Experiences	Lieketseng
Ideas	Makhopo
Perception	Polelo Ka
Personality	Motho Motho
Problem	Bothata
Reality	Sebele
Sensation	Tšebeletso
Therapy	Pheko
Thoughts	Likeletso
Unconscious	Tlhokomeliso

Rainforest
Meru ea Pula

Birds	Linonyana
Climate	Lesotho
Clouds	Maru
Community	Sechaba
Diversity	Fapaneng
Indigenous	Mots'Oaoa
Insects	Likhoane
Jungle	Sehlabane
Mammals	Linyama
Moss	Moso
Nature	Tlhaho
Preservation	Paballo
Refuge	Ts'Ababelo
Respect	Hlompho
Restoration	Puseletso
Species	Litšoantšiso
Survival	Pholoa
Valuable	Bohlokoa

Restaurant #1
Lebenkele #1

Allergy	Tlhokomeliso
Bowl	Sekopi
Bread	Bohobe
Cashier	Mokhethi
Chicken	Khoho
Coffee	Kofi
Dessert	Lets'Elisi
Food	Lijo
Ingredients	Lieketseng
Kitchen	Tsietsi
Knife	Thipa
Meat	Khoma
Menu	Menu
Napkin	Napkin
Reservation	Peketso
Sauce	Soso
Spicy	Linako
Waitress	Mots'Elisi

Restaurant #2
Lebenkele #2

Cake	Keke
Chair	Ts'Eliso
Delicious	Thabeleng
Dinner	Tšebeletso
Eggs	Mahe
Fish	Lihlapi
Fork	Pheko
Fruit	Tholoana
Ice	Leqetsa
Lunch	Tšebeletso
Noodles	Limane
Salad	Salate
Salt	Letswai
Soup	Sopo
Spices	Linko
Spoon	Khabane
Vegetables	Merotso
Waiter	Mothusi
Water	Metsi

Science
Saense

Atom	Atom
Chemical	K'Hemik'Hale
Climate	Lesotho
Data	Data
Evolution	Phetohoa
Experiment	Lekeletso
Fact	Sebele
Fossil	Mohlala
Gravity	Khoheli
Laboratory	Laboratori
Method	Mokhoa
Minerals	Lits'Epa
Molecules	Molek'Hue
Nature	Tlhaho
Observation	Tebello
Organism	Ts'Epa
Particles	Lieketseng
Physics	Fihla
Plants	Limela
Scientist	Mots'Eane

Science Fiction
Lingoloa tsa Boiqapelo T

Atomic	Atomo
Books	Libuka
Chemicals	Limakase
Cinema	Khahliso
Dystopia	Dystopia
Explosion	Puseletso
Extreme	Khabane
Fantastic	Ts'Elisitsoe
Fire	Mollo
Futuristic	Futuristi
Galaxy	Khalaxe
Illusion	Tsietso
Imaginary	Ts'Oalang
Mysterious	Mohlomi
Oracle	Oracle
Planet	Planete
Robots	Liroboto
Technology	Theknoloji
Utopia	Utopia
World	Lefatshe

Scientific Disciplines
Litaelo tsa Saense

Anatomy	Anatome
Archaeology	Tšepo
Astronomy	Ts'Oanelo
Biology	Ts'Epo
Botany	Botanyane
Chemistry	Khemithi
Geology	Geoloji
Immunology	Mots'Oaoa
Kinesiology	Kinesioloji
Linguistics	Lipuo
Mechanics	Lieketseng
Meteorology	Boemoholo
Mineralogy	Mineralogo
Nutrition	Phepo
Physics	Fihla
Physiology	Phiriloe
Psychology	Ts'Ehloko
Robotics	Liroboto
Sociology	Tšebeletso
Zoology	Tšoolo

Shapes
Libopeho

Arc	Arc
Cone	Kona
Corner	Sek'Ona
Cube	Cube
Cylinder	Motsamai
Edges	Matšoele
Ellipse	Ellipse
Hyperbola	Moholo Oa
Line	Mokhoa
Oval	Oval
Polygon	Polyone
Prism	Prism
Pyramid	Pyramid
Rectangle	Khabane
Side	Lehlakoana
Sphere	Sebaka
Square	Lekakare
Triangle	Ts'Eliso

Spices
Linoko

Anise	Anise
Bitter	Bohloko
Cardamom	Karete
Cinnamon	Kinamo
Clove	Lets'Oane
Coriander	Koriande
Cumin	Cumin
Curry	Khara
Fennel	Fennel
Flavor	Tamano
Garlic	Konofole
Ginger	Thamana
Licorice	Likopo
Nutmeg	Nutmeg
Onion	Anyanese
Paprika	Paprika
Saffron	Safronike
Salt	Letswai
Sweet	Monate
Vanilla	Vanila

Sport
Lipapali

Ability	Bokhopo
Athlete	Moathibeli
Body	Mmele
Bones	Masapo
Cardiovascular	Khadiovascula
Cycling	Baekela
Dancing	Motsamai
Diet	Jeso
Endurance	Mamello
Goal	Sepheo
Health	Pholoso
Jogging	Tšebeletso
Maximize	Moeketsi
Metabolic	Motboli
Muscles	Masiri
Nutrition	Phepo
Program	Lenaneo
Sports	Lipapali
Strength	Matla

The Company
Khamphani

Business	Khoebo
Creative	Mokhopo
Decision	Qeto
Employment	Mosebetsi
Global	Lefatshe
Industry	Indakane
Innovative	Ts'Oanelo
Investment	Petetso
Possibility	Mokhoamo
Presentation	Tlhokomelo
Product	Product
Professional	Motsamai
Progress	Tsoelo-Pele
Quality	Khabane
Reputation	Tšebeletso
Revenue	Leketso
Risks	Likotsi
Trends	Lits'Eliso
Units	Lieketseng
Wages	Moputso

Time
Nako

Before	Pele
Calendar	Khalenda
Century	Lekholhooa
Clock	Tšebele
Day	Letsatsi
Decade	Selemo
Early	Tsohle
Future	Bokamoso
Hour	Hora
Minute	Motsotso
Month	Khoeli
Morning	Moso
Night	Bosiu
Noon	Motšebele
Now	Hona Joale
Soon	Haufinyane
Today	Ts'Oanelo
Week	Beketso
Year	Selemo
Yesterday	Maobane

Town
Toropo

Airport	Sefofa
Bakery	Bakereke
Bank	Banka
Cinema	Khahliso
Clinic	Kliniki
Florist	Palesa
Gallery	Khalele
Hotel	Hotele
Library	Moeketsi
Market	Mareka
Museum	Musemo
Pharmacy	Phakamasi
School	Sekolo
Stadium	Stadium
Store	Lebekeng
Supermarket	Supamakete
Theater	Tšebeletso
University	Univesite
Zoo	Zoo

Universe
Bokahohle

Asteroid	Asteroid
Astronomer	Mohlankanyane
Astronomy	Ts'Oanelo
Atmosphere	Sebaka
Celestial	Leholimo
Cosmic	Khotso
Darkness	Lefifi
Equator	Equator
Galaxy	Khalaxe
Hemisphere	Khabane
Horizon	Ts'Eliso
Latitude	Leboko
Moon	Khoeli
Orbit	Tsela
Sky	Sekopi
Solar	Hlalele
Solstice	Tlhokomeliso
Telescope	Thelesekopo
Visible	Bonahala
Zodiac	Zodiac

Vacation #2
Phomolo #2

Airport	Sefofa
Beach	Leboteng
Camping	Motsamai
Destination	Lebaka
Foreigner	Mochaba
Holiday	Phomolo
Hotel	Hotele
Island	Sehlakane
Journey	Leeto
Leisure	Ts'Eliso
Map	Map
Mountains	Lithabeng
Passport	Paseka
Photos	Litšoantšo
Sea	Leoatla
Taxi	Tekesi
Tent	Tenteng
Train	Thuto
Transportation	Tsamai
Visa	Visa

Vegetables
Meroho

Artichoke	Artichoke
Broccoli	Broccoli
Carrot	Sehoete
Cauliflower	Kholifolaoa
Celery	Seleri
Cucumber	Komokomore
Eggplant	Eggplant
Garlic	Konofole
Ginger	Thamana
Mushroom	Mushroom
Onion	Anyanese
Parsley	Parsle
Pea	Pea
Pumpkin	Mokopu
Radish	Radise
Salad	Salate
Shallot	Shallot
Spinach	Sepinichi
Tomato	Tamati
Turnip	Thibaka

Vehicles
Likoloi

Airplane	Sefofane
Ambulance	Ambulese
Bicycle	Baekela
Boat	Sekepe
Bus	Bese
Caravan	Koloi
Engine	Ts'Oane
Ferry	Moeketsi
Helicopter	Helikopele
Motor	Motsamai
Raft	Raft
Rocket	Rokete
Scooter	Sekokota
Submarine	Ts'Eliso
Taxi	Tekesi
Tires	Lieketseng
Tractor	Tebiri
Train	Thuto
Truck	Tereka
Van	Van

Visual Arts
Bonono ba Pono

Artist	Moeketsi
Ceramics	Liekeremere
Chalk	Khahle
Charcoal	Leshala
Clay	Letsopa
Composition	Motsamai
Creativity	Tlhokomeliso
Easel	Easel
Film	Fihla
Masterpiece	Seemahale
Painting	Peko
Pen	Pen
Pencil	Pensele
Perspective	Pono Potso
Photograph	Sefoto
Portrait	Setšoantšo
Sculpture	Sets'Oaoa
Stencil	Stensele
Wax	Kaka

Water
Metsi

Canal	Kananelo
Damp	Letšela
Evaporation	Mofoufu
Flood	Kholala
Frost	Setsane
Geyser	Geyser
Humidity	Monate
Hurricane	Lets'Oane
Ice	Leqetsa
Irrigation	Ts'Eliso
Lake	Letšetše
Moisture	Mosola
Monsoon	Mohlomi
Ocean	Leoetle
Rain	Puleng
River	Molapo
Shower	Hlats'A
Snow	Lehloenya
Steam	Steam
Waves	Matsoso

Weather
Boemo ba Leholimo

Atmosphere	Sebaka
Breeze	Motsamai
Calm	Tsietso
Climate	Lesotho
Cloud	Leruu
Drought	Komelo
Dry	Ometsa
Fog	Fogane
Hurricane	Lets'Oane
Ice	Leqetsa
Lightning	Motlatsi
Monsoon	Mohlomi
Polar	Polar
Rainbow	Molemotsi
Sky	Sekopi
Storm	Sefefo
Thunder	Seaduma
Tornado	Sehlokoane
Tropical	Tšebeletso
Wind	Phefo

Congratulations

You made it!

We hope you enjoyed this book as much as we enjoyed making it. We do our best to make high quality games.
These puzzles are designed in a clever way for you to learn actively while having fun!

Did you love them?

A Simple Request

Our books exist thanks your reviews. Could you help us by leaving one now?

Here is a short link which will take you to your order review page:

BestBooksActivity.com/Review50

MONSTER CHALLENGE!

Challenge #1

Ready for Your Bonus Game? We use them all the time but they are not so easy to find. Here are **Synonyms**!

Note 5 words you discovered in each of the Puzzles noted below (#21, #36, #76) and try to find 2 synonyms for each word.

Note 5 Words from *Puzzle 21*

Words	Synonym 1	Synonym 2

Note 5 Words from *Puzzle 36*

Words	Synonym 1	Synonym 2

Note 5 Words from *Puzzle 76*

Words	Synonym 1	Synonym 2

Challenge #2

Now that you are warmed-up, note 5 words you discovered in each Puzzle noted below (#9, #17, #25) and try to find 2 antonyms for each word. How many lines can you do in 20 minutes?

Note 5 Words from **Puzzle 9**

Words	Antonym 1	Antonym 2

Note 5 Words from **Puzzle 17**

Words	Antonym 1	Antonym 2

Note 5 Words from **Puzzle 25**

Words	Antonym 1	Antonym 2

Challenge #3

Wonderful, this monster   challenge is nothing to you!

Ready for the last one? Choose your 10 favorite words discovered in any of the Puzzles and note them below.

1.	6.
2.	7.
3.	8.
4.	9.
5.	10.

Now, using these words and within a maximum of six sentences, your challenge is to compose a text about a person, animal or place that you love!

Tip: You can use the last blank page of this book as a draft!

Your Writing:

Explore a Unique Store
Set Up **FOR YOU!**

MEGA DEALS

BestActivityBooks.com/**TheStore**

Designed for Entertainment!

Light Up Your Brain With Unique **Gift Ideas**.

Access **Surprising** And **Essential Supplies!**

CHECK OUT OUR MONTHLY SELECTION NOW!

- Expertly Crafted Products -

NOTEBOOK:

SEE YOU SOON!

Linguas Classics Team

BESTACTIVITYBOOKS.COM/FREEGAMES